ZENTANTLE CREATIONS

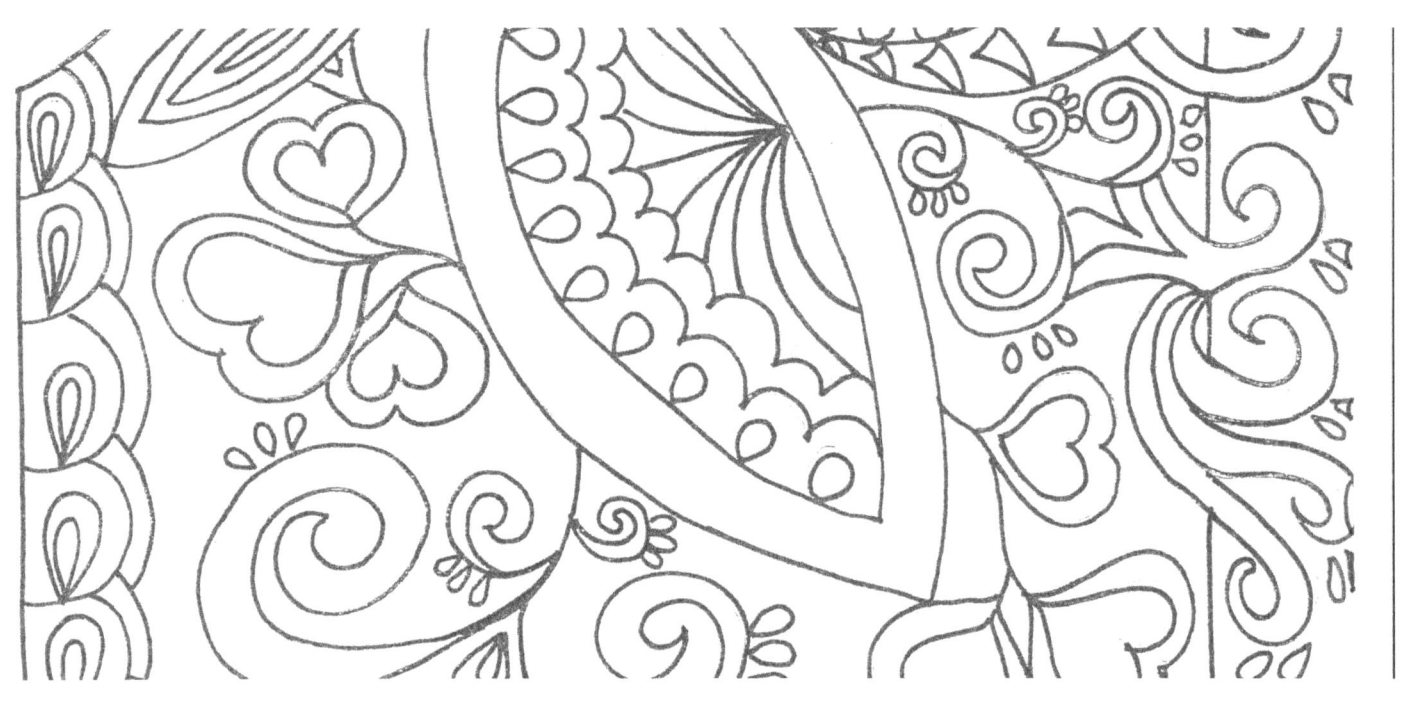

ELAYNE TENNANT

VOLUME. 1

INTRODUCTION

I have enjoyed creating this wonderful and relaxing coloring book for all of you who like to lose yourself and become stress free in the art of coloring. I am an Artist of many mediums from painting to drawing and love the world of abstract, in this book you will find the integration of abstracts and Zentangle. Releasing this first Volume is the first step into many more coloring books to be created with only my original drawings and imagination.

Creating a world or drawings to lose yourself in and finding the relaxing mindlessness of coloring these beautiful pages of art as a calming therapeutic way to release tensions from the outside world.

I hope that you find this coloring book to be a relaxing part of your life as I did while creating it for you.

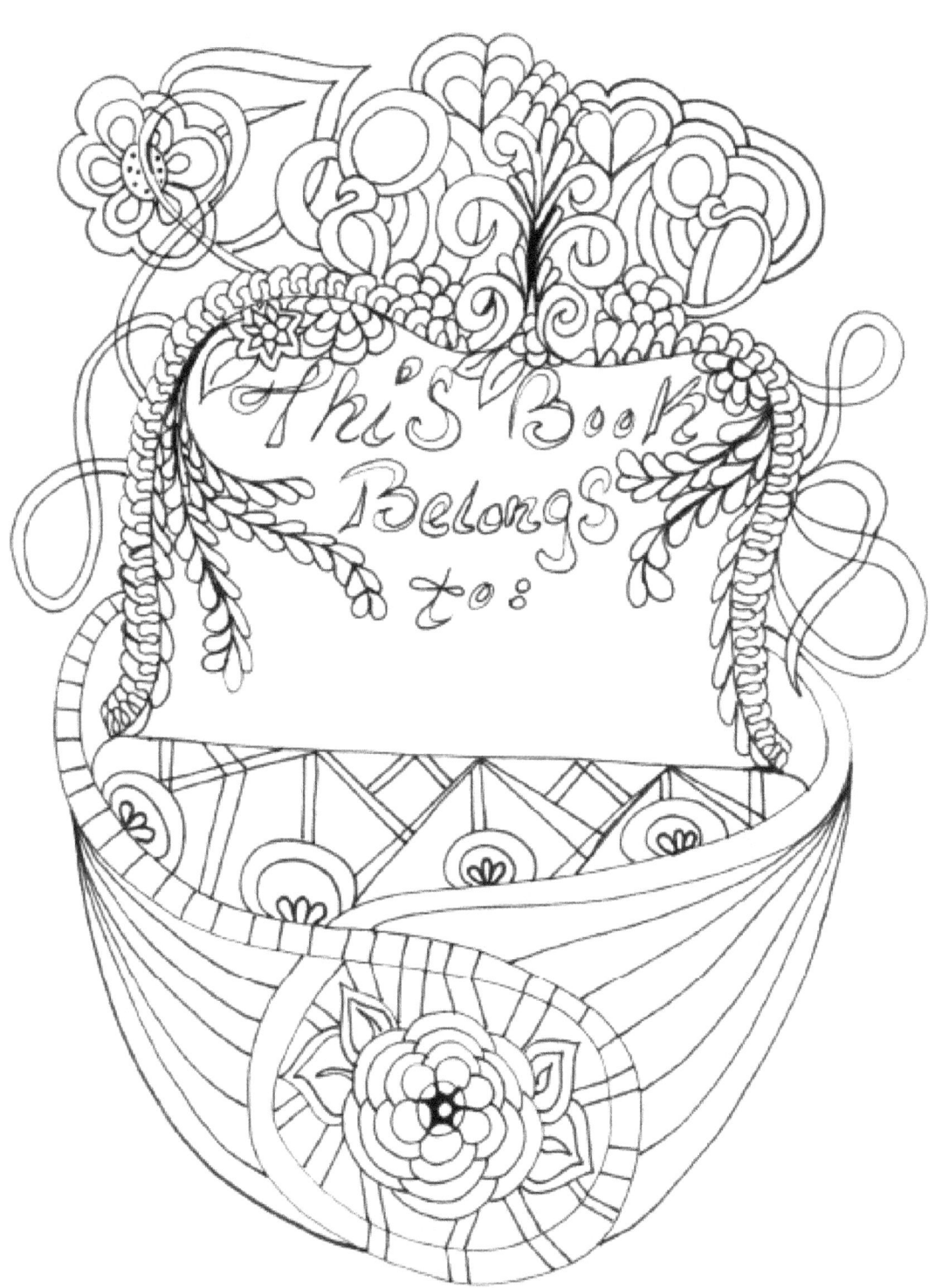

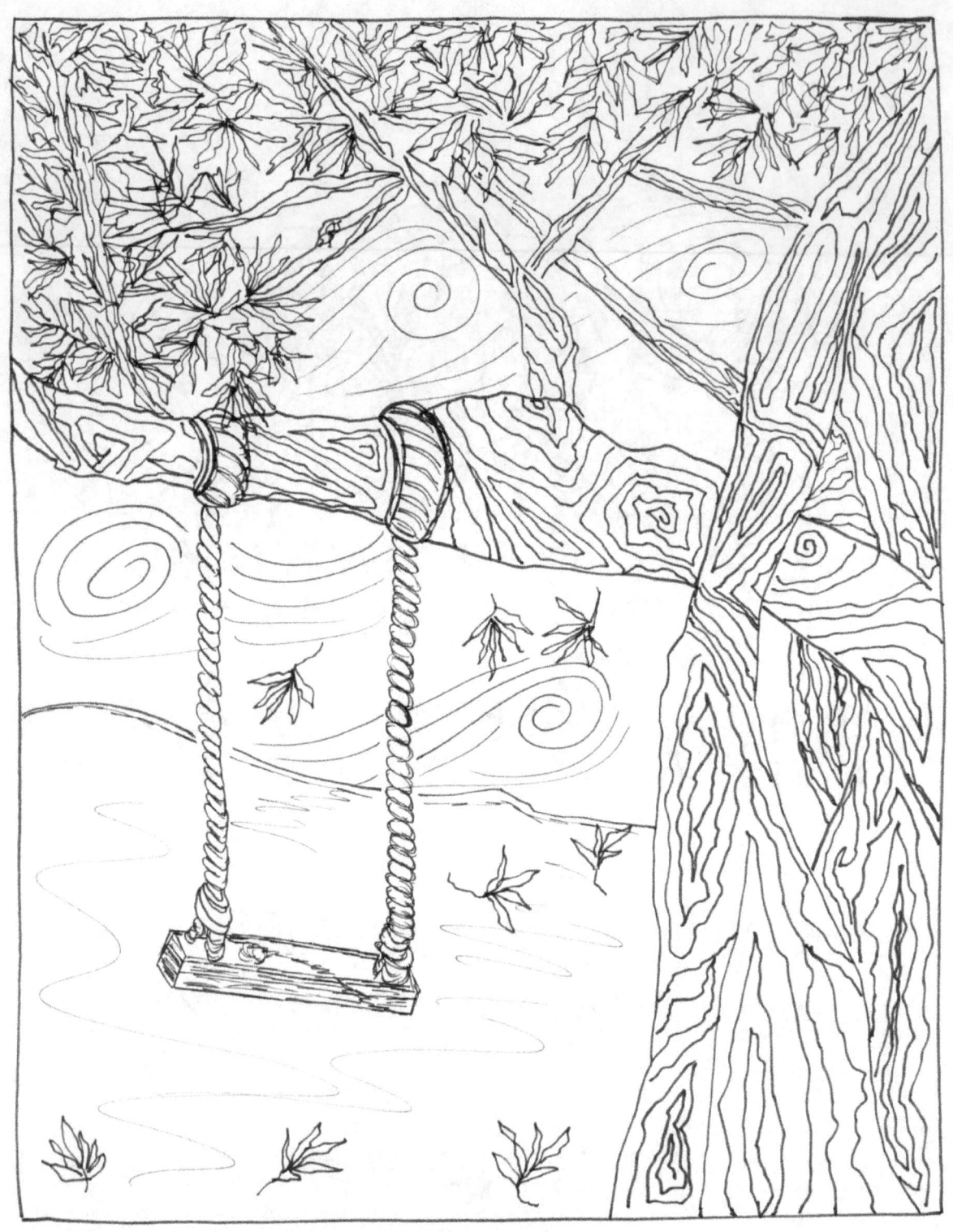

BLUSTERY DAY

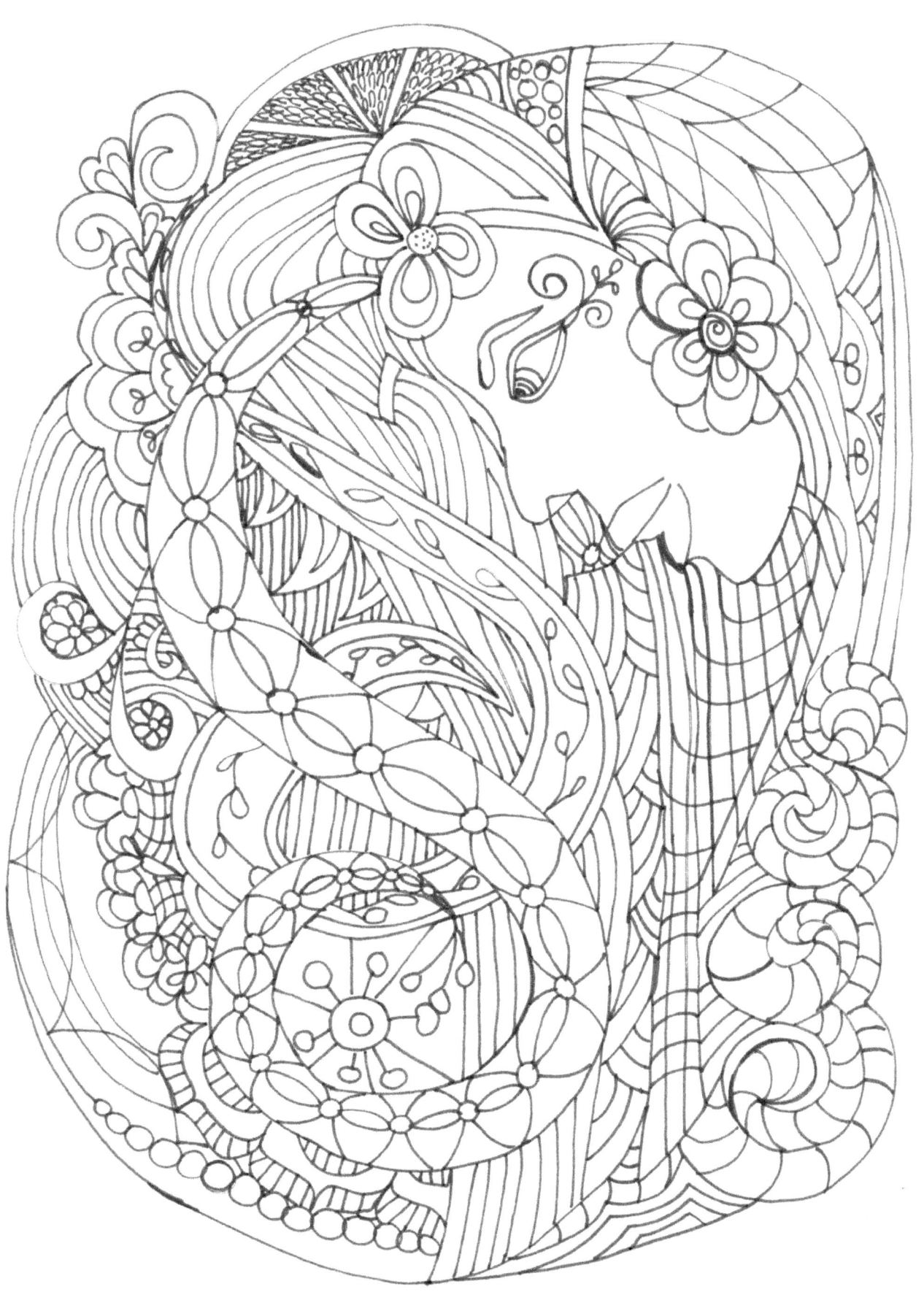

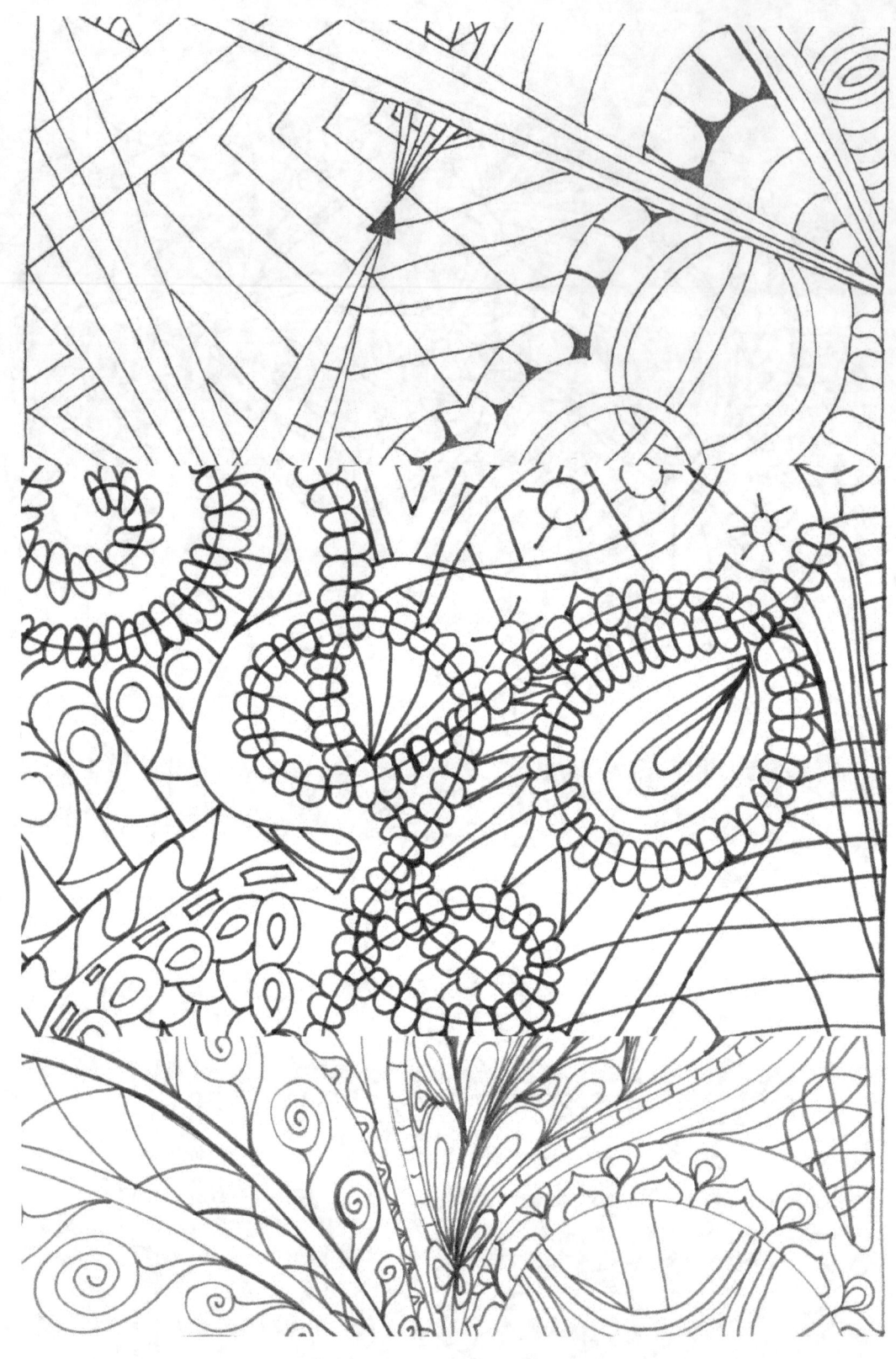

KEEP IT SIMPLE AND COLORFUL

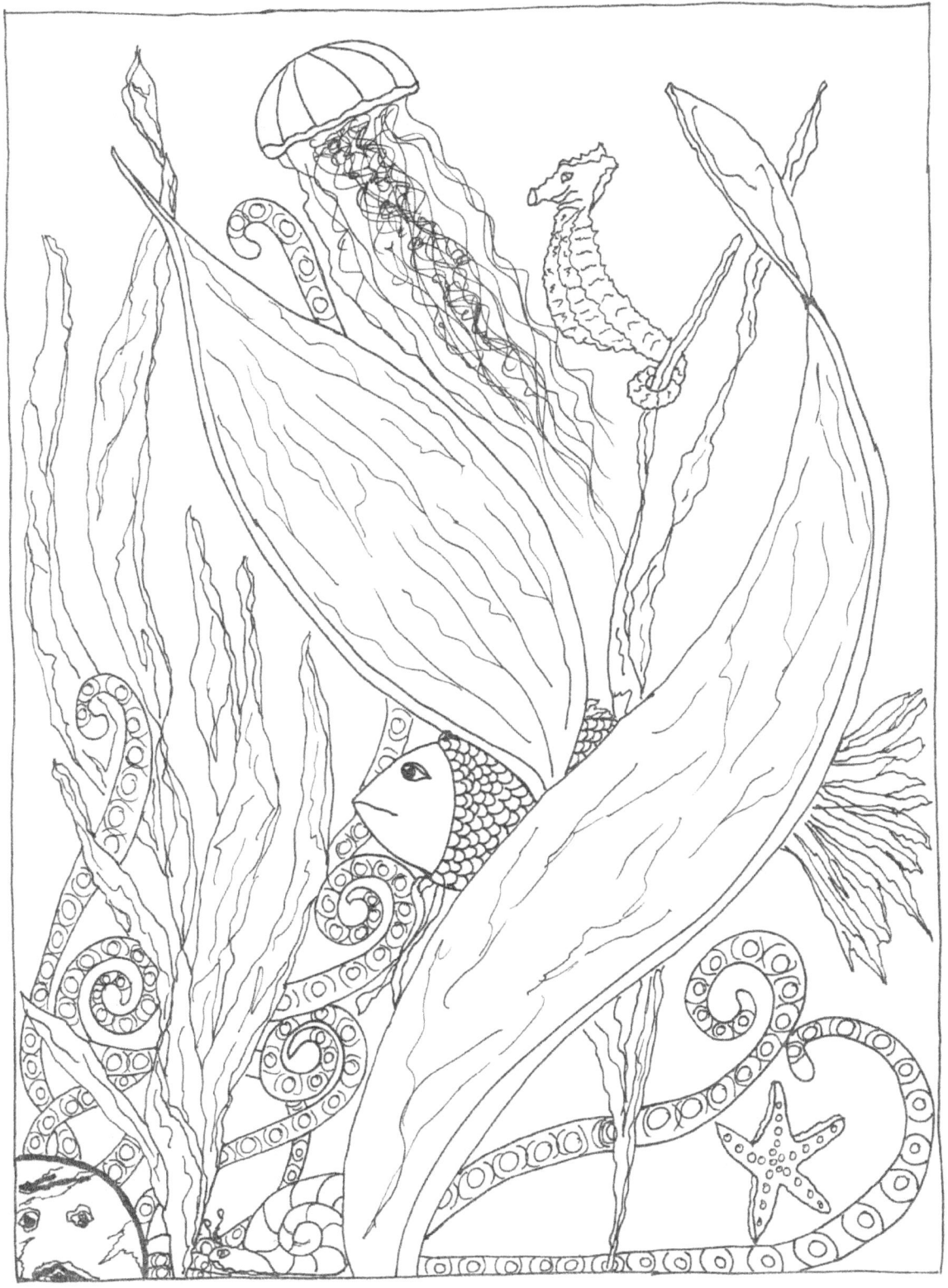

SIMPLY LOVING LIFE

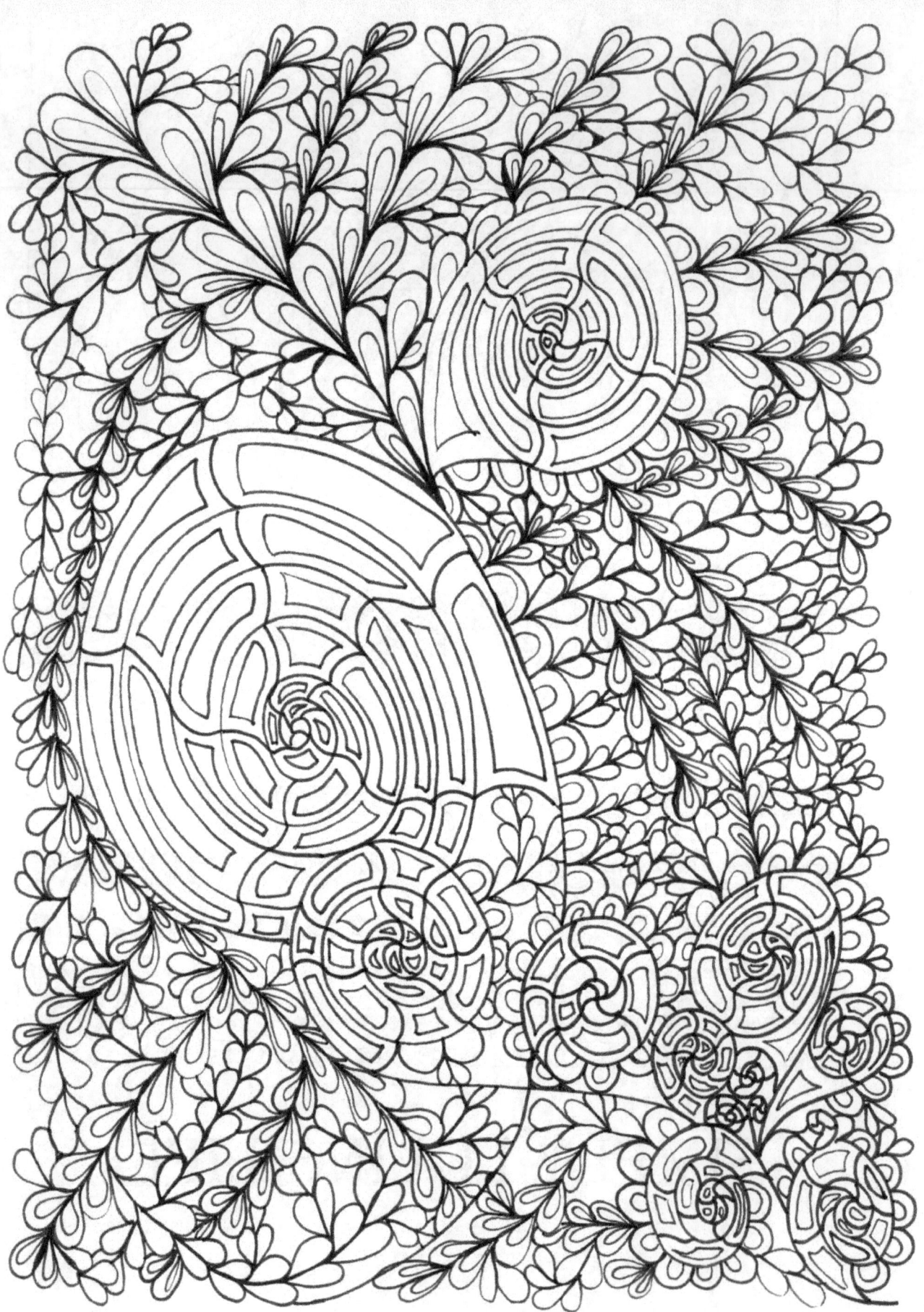

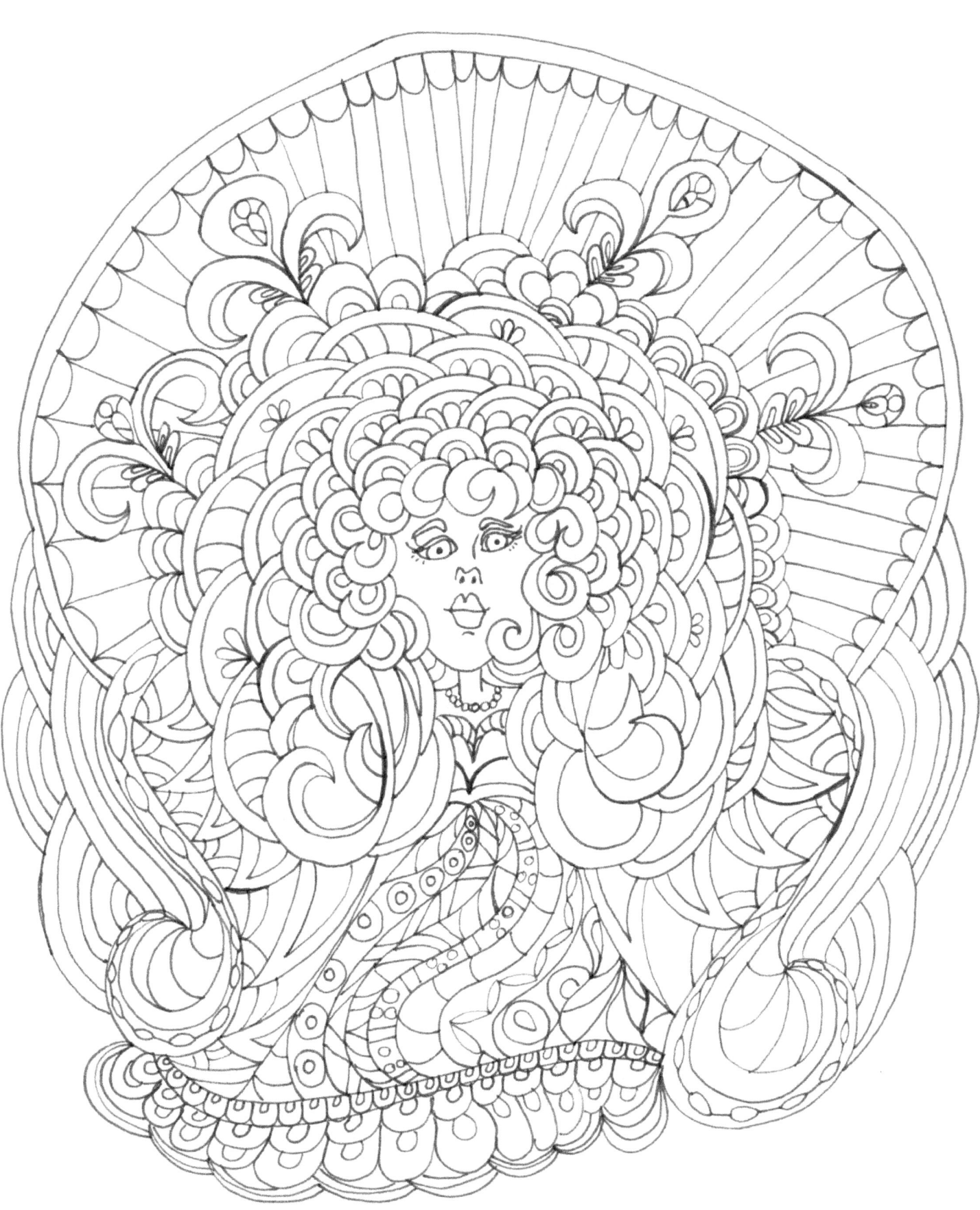

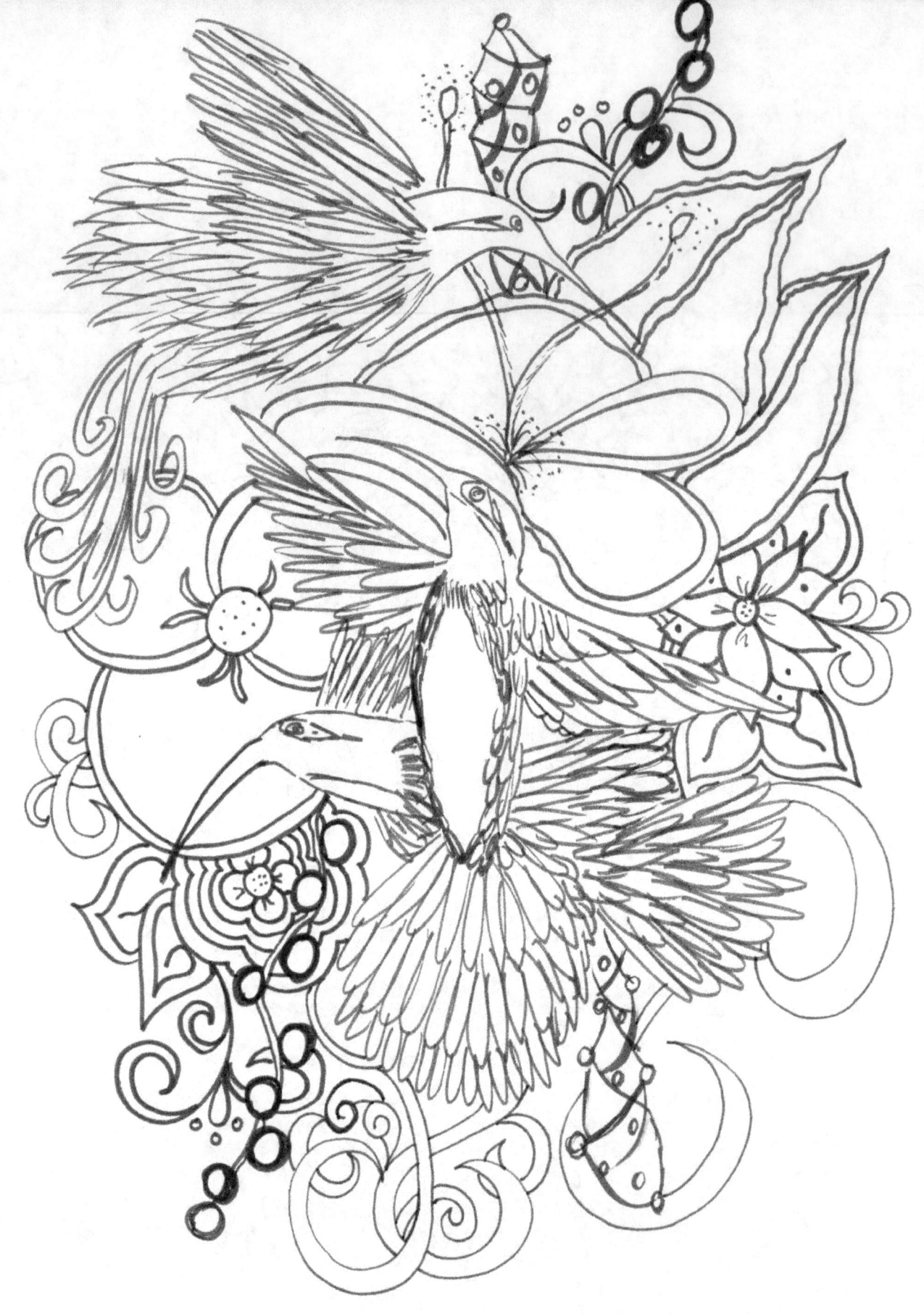

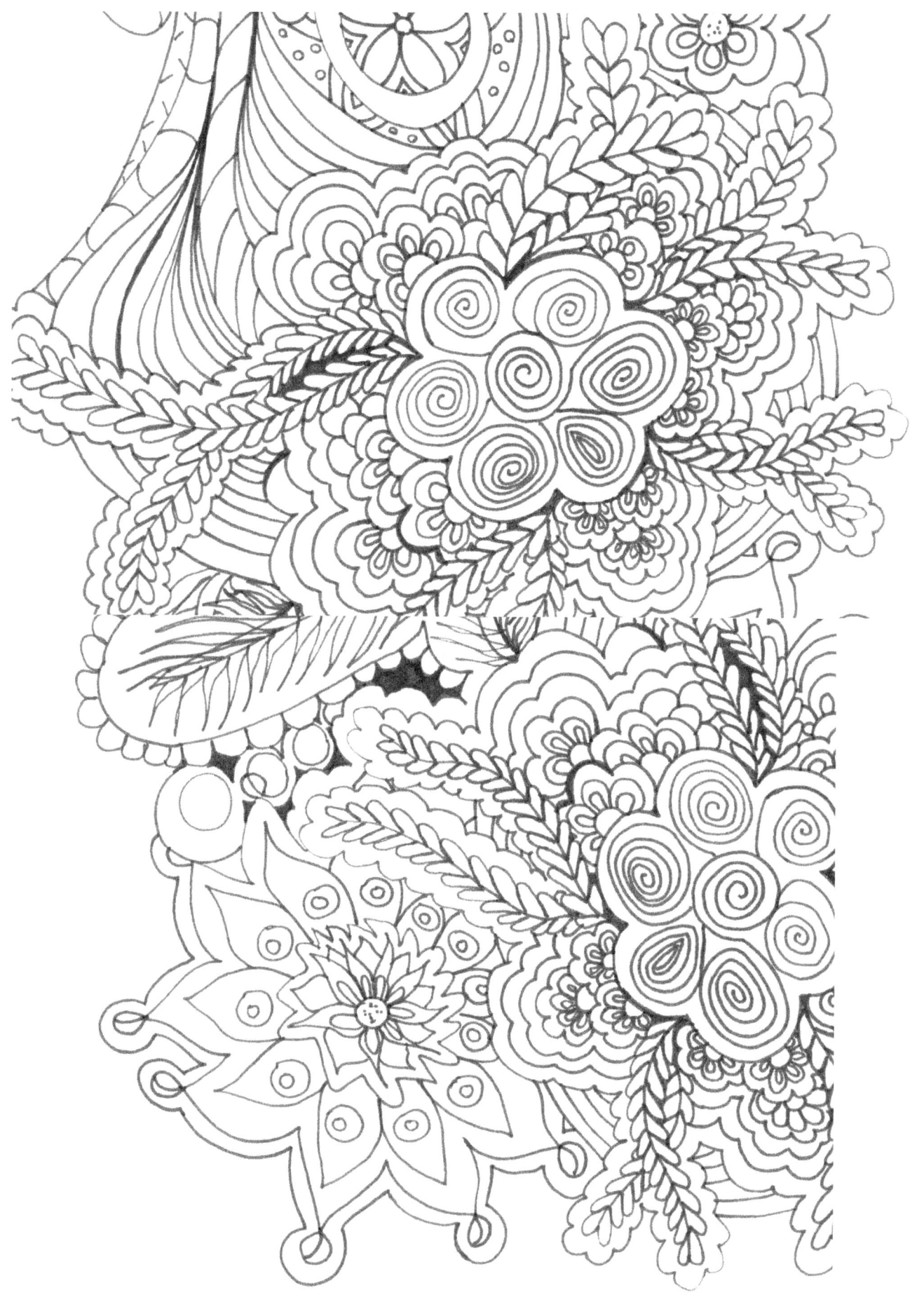

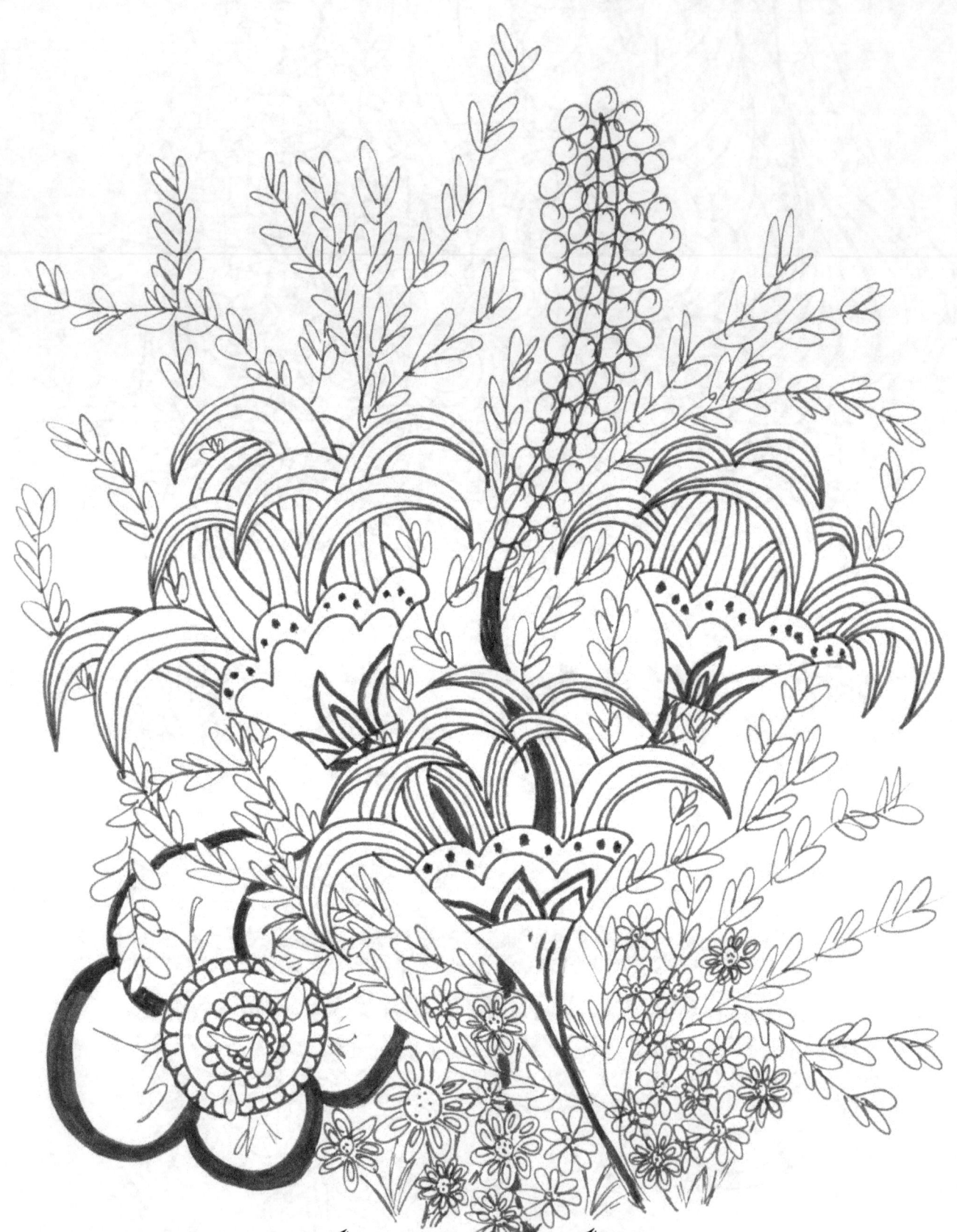

CREATE YOUR OWN BEAUTIFUL GARDEN

NAMESTE

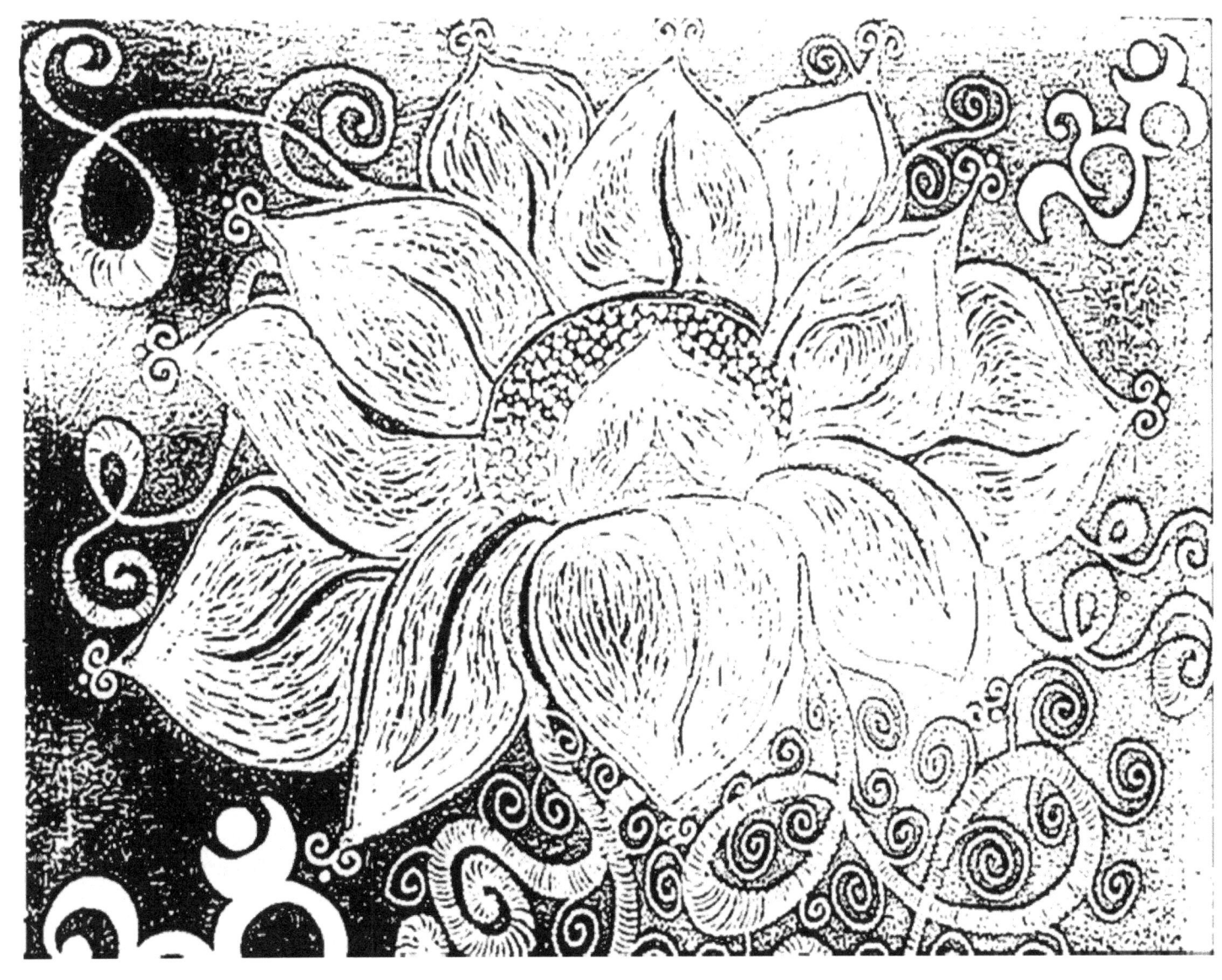

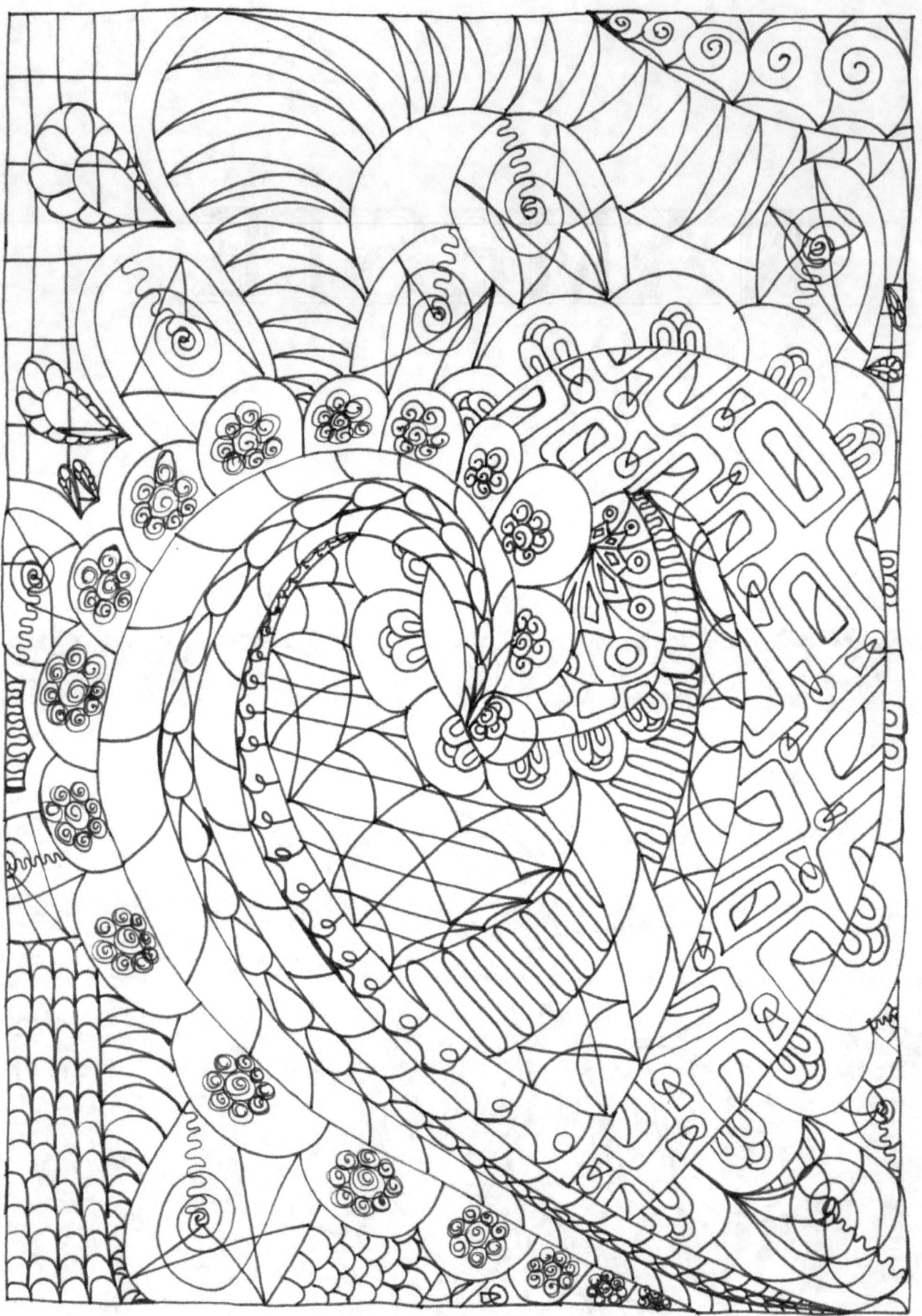

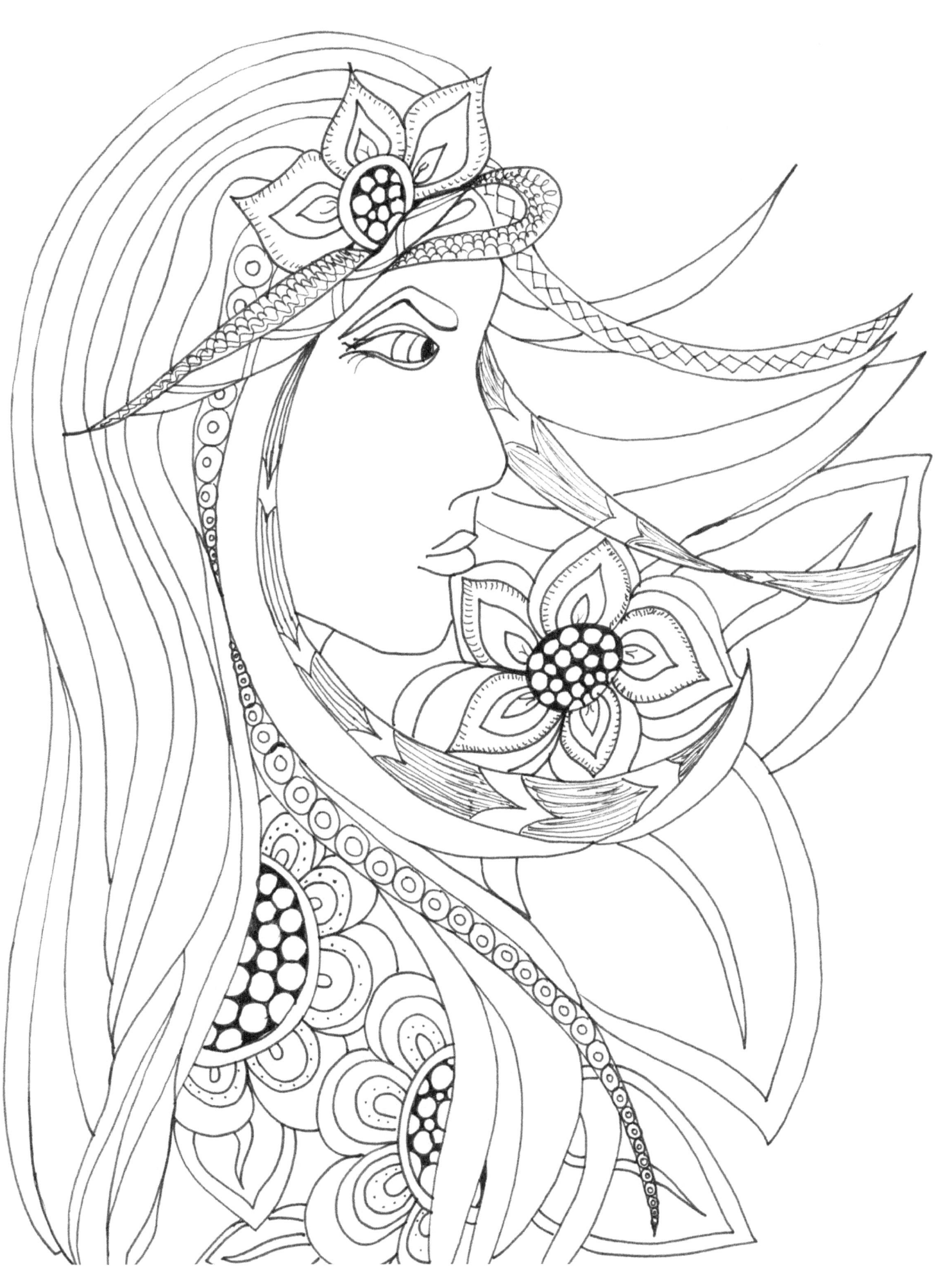

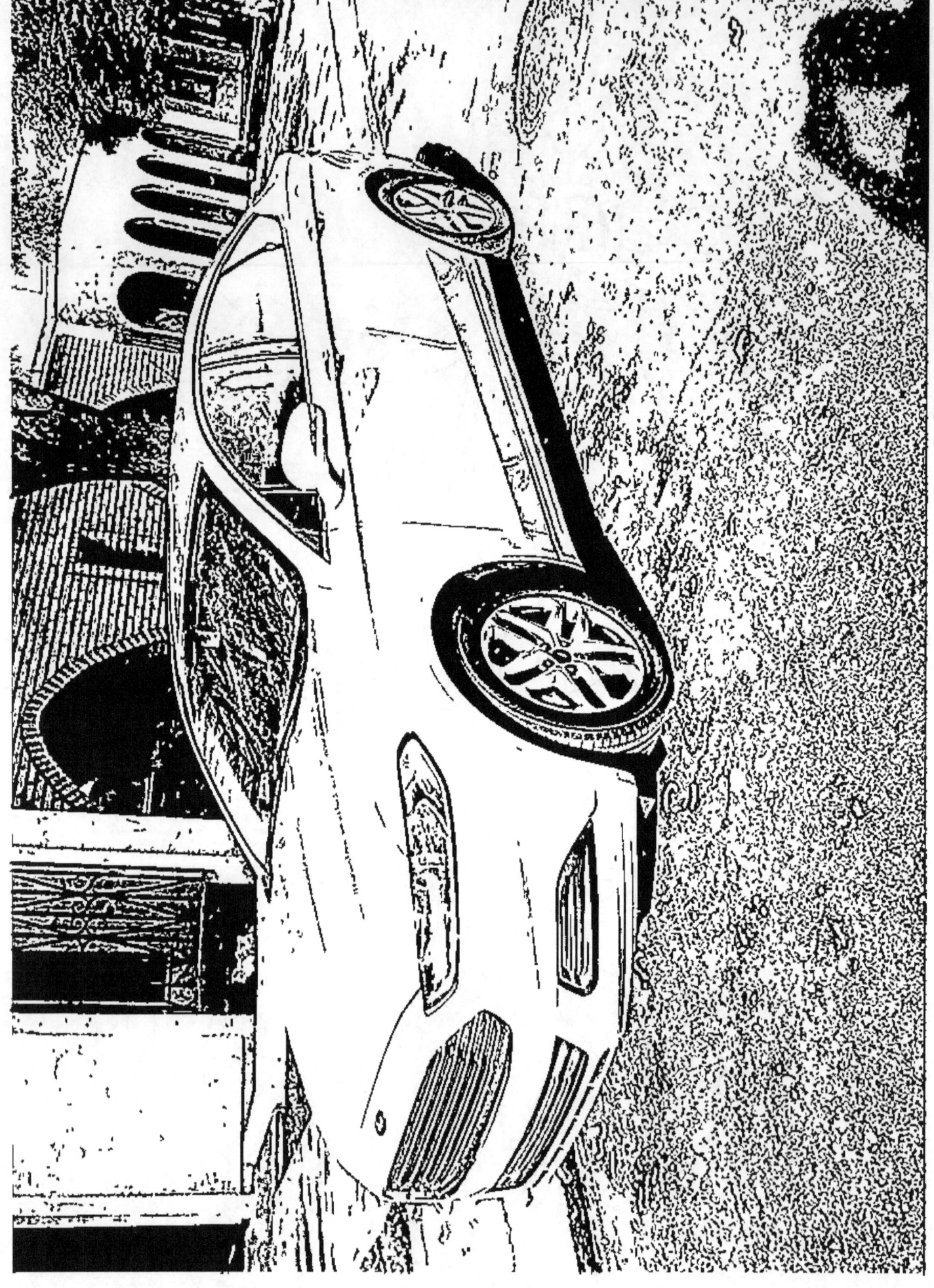

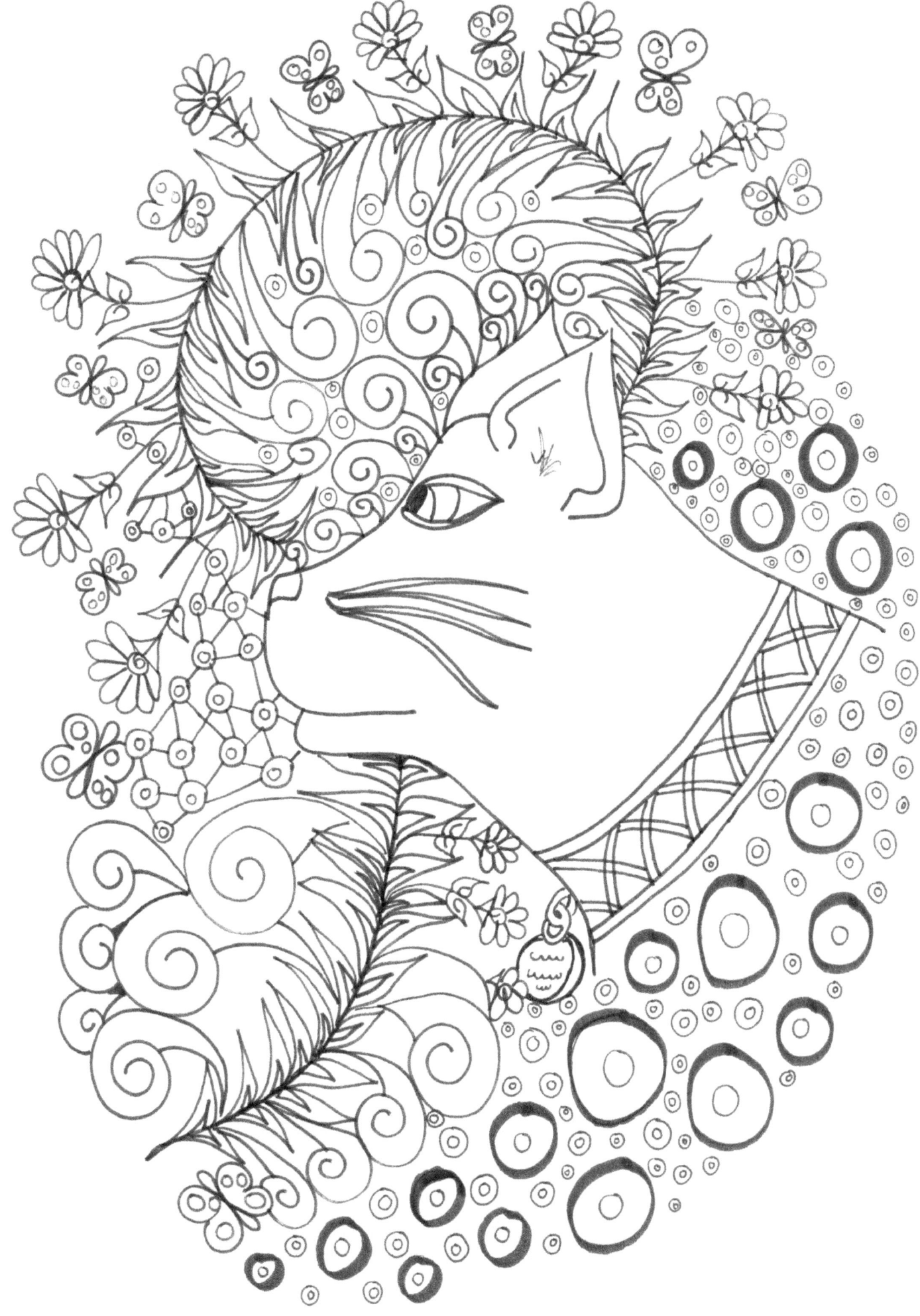

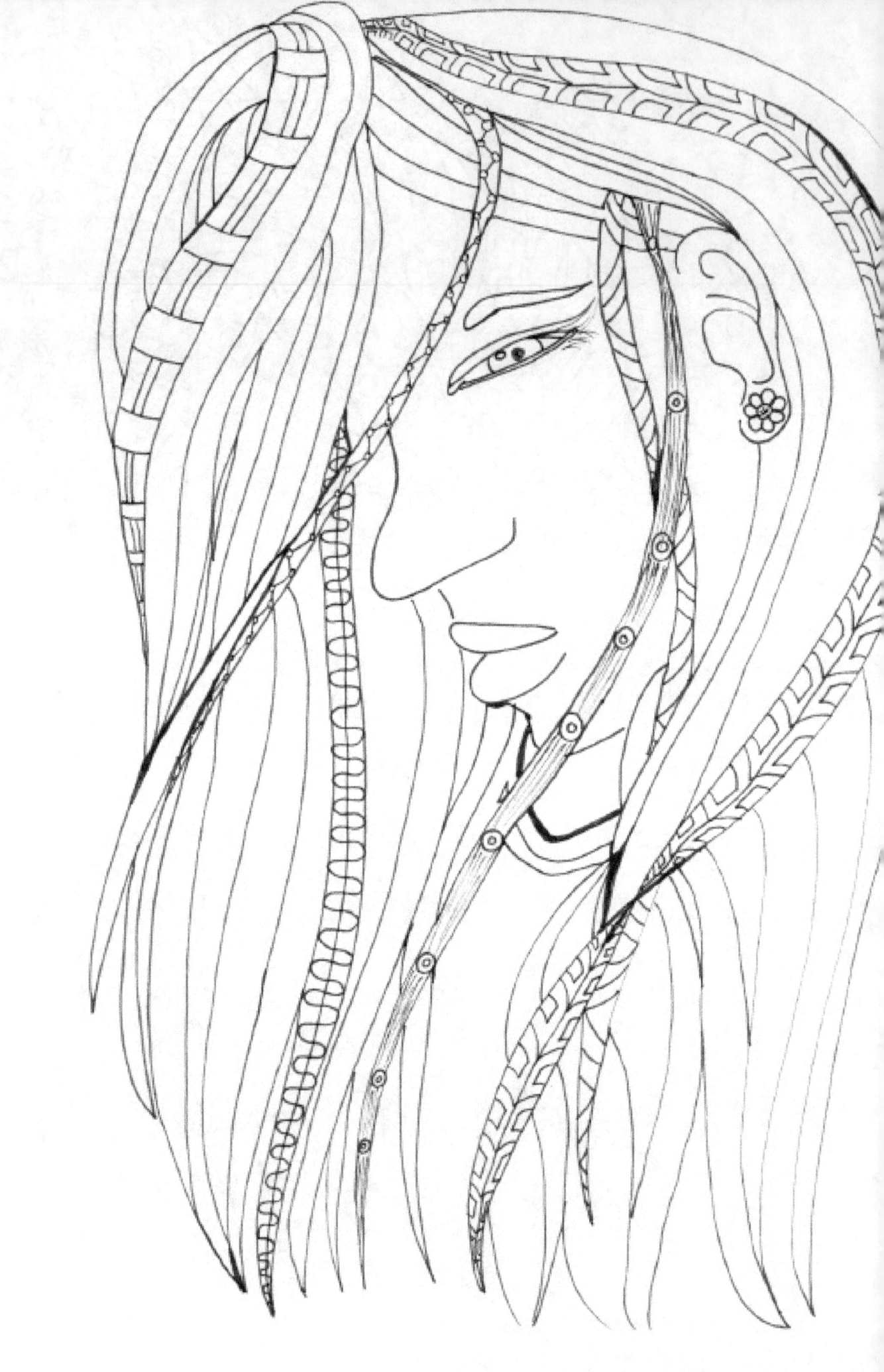

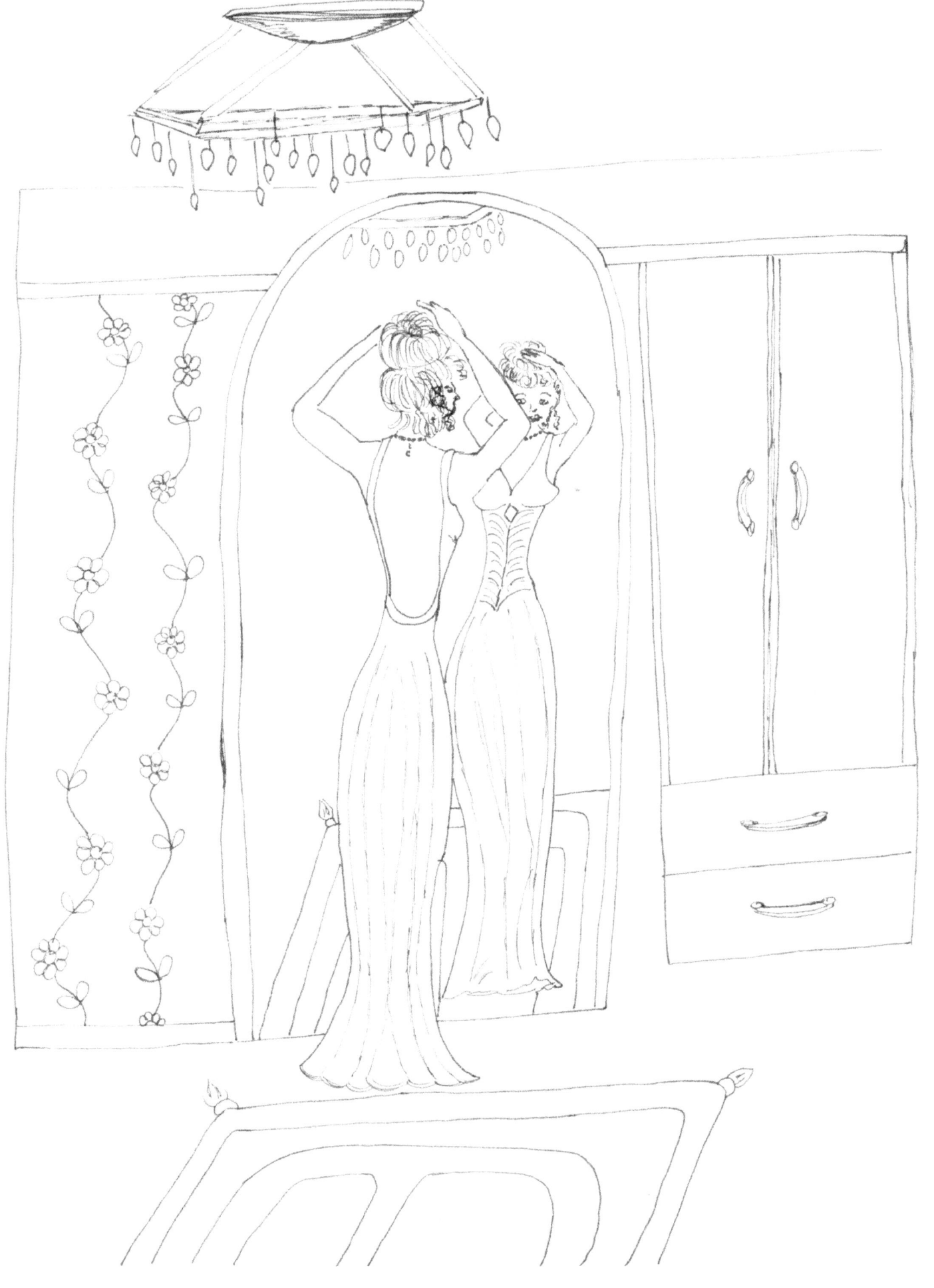

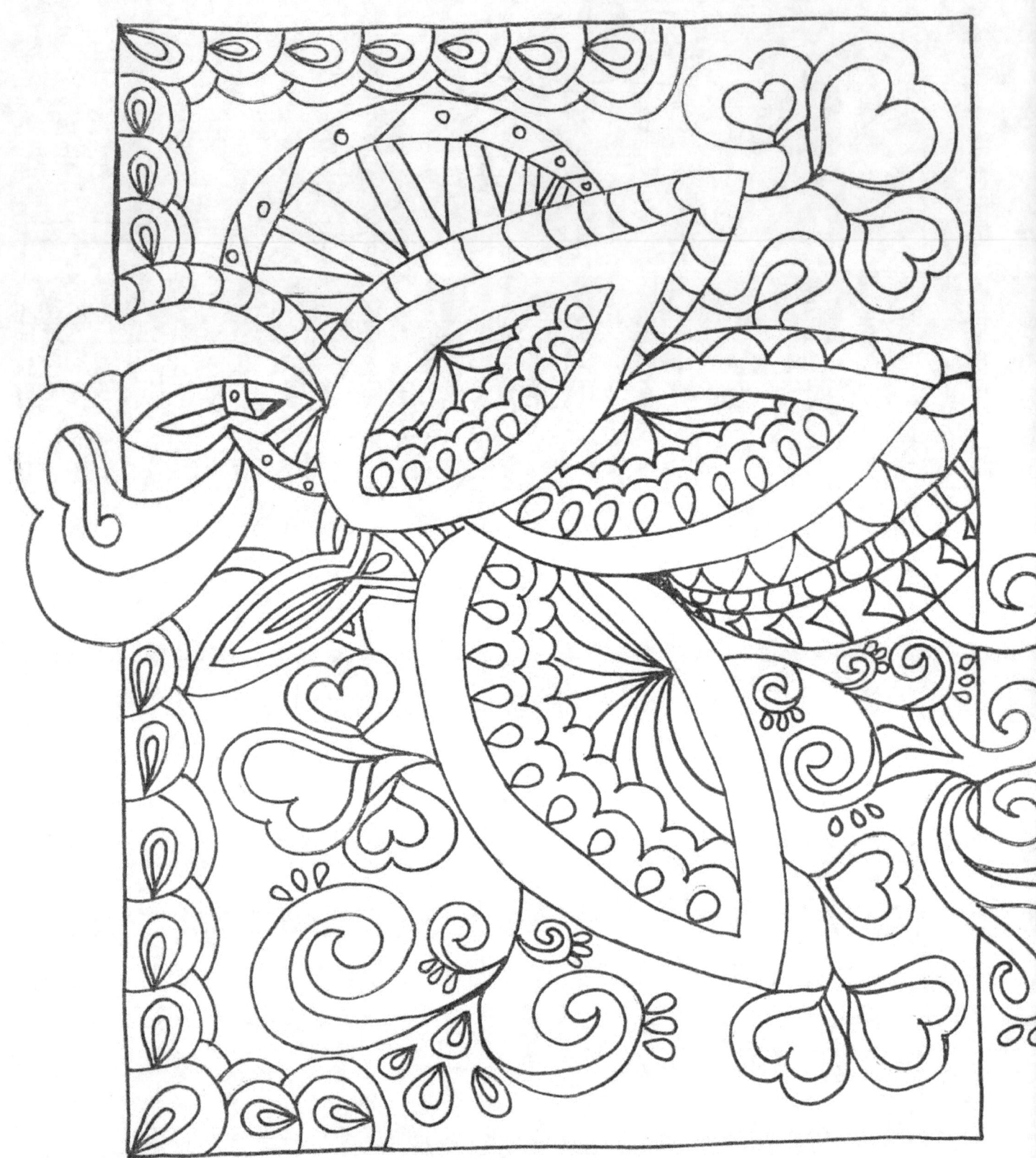

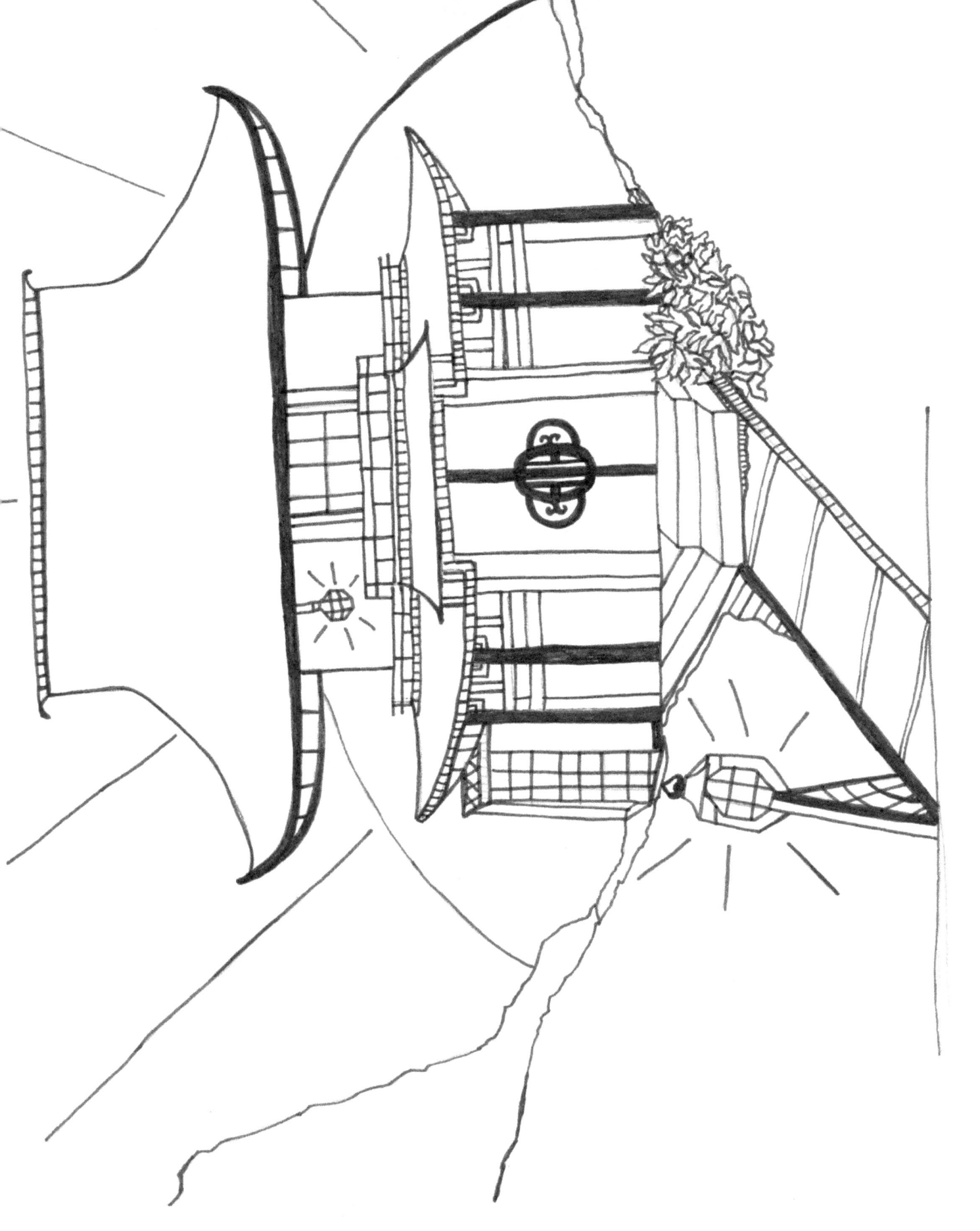

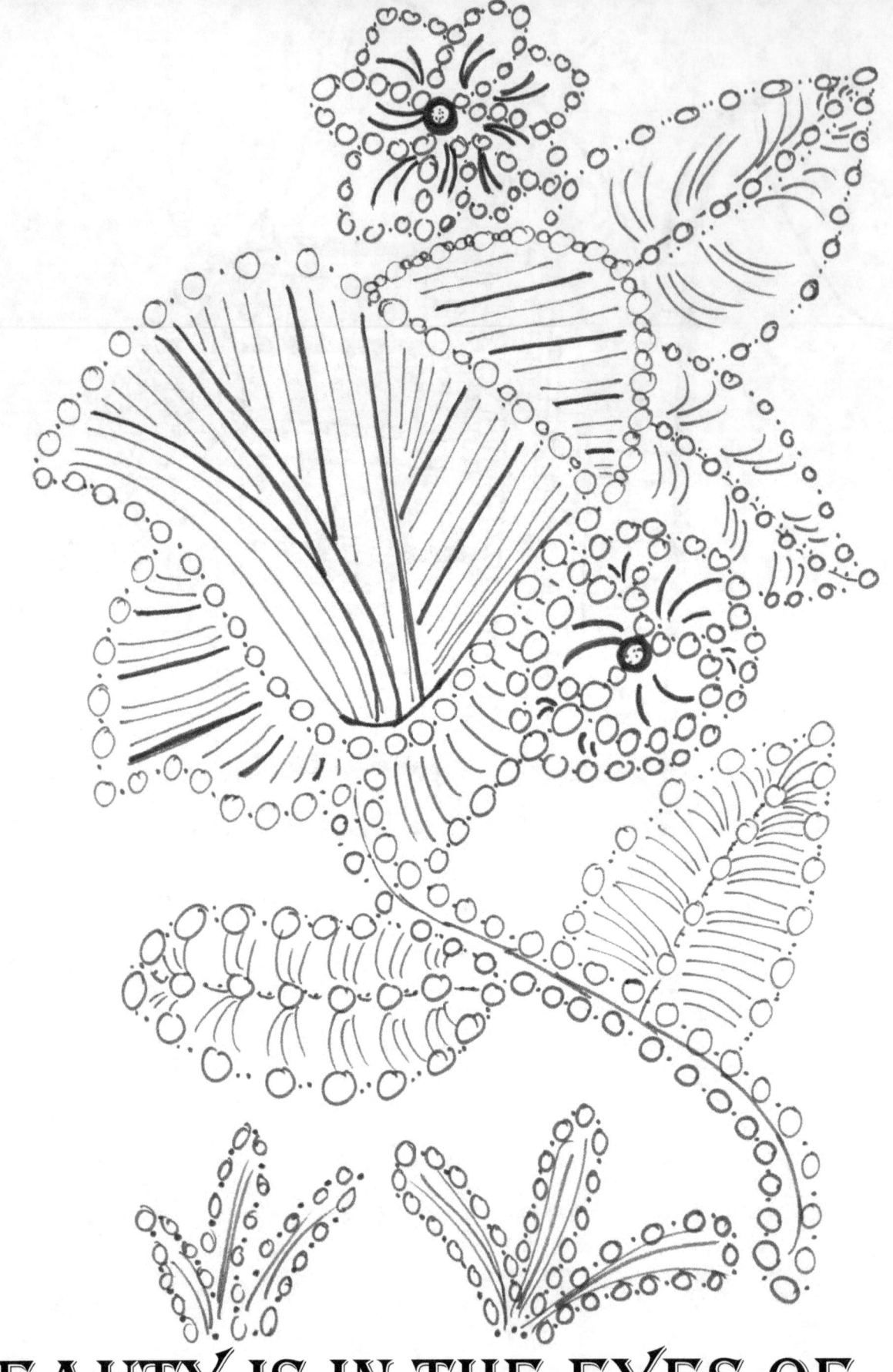

BEAUTY IS IN THE EYES OF THE BEHOLDER

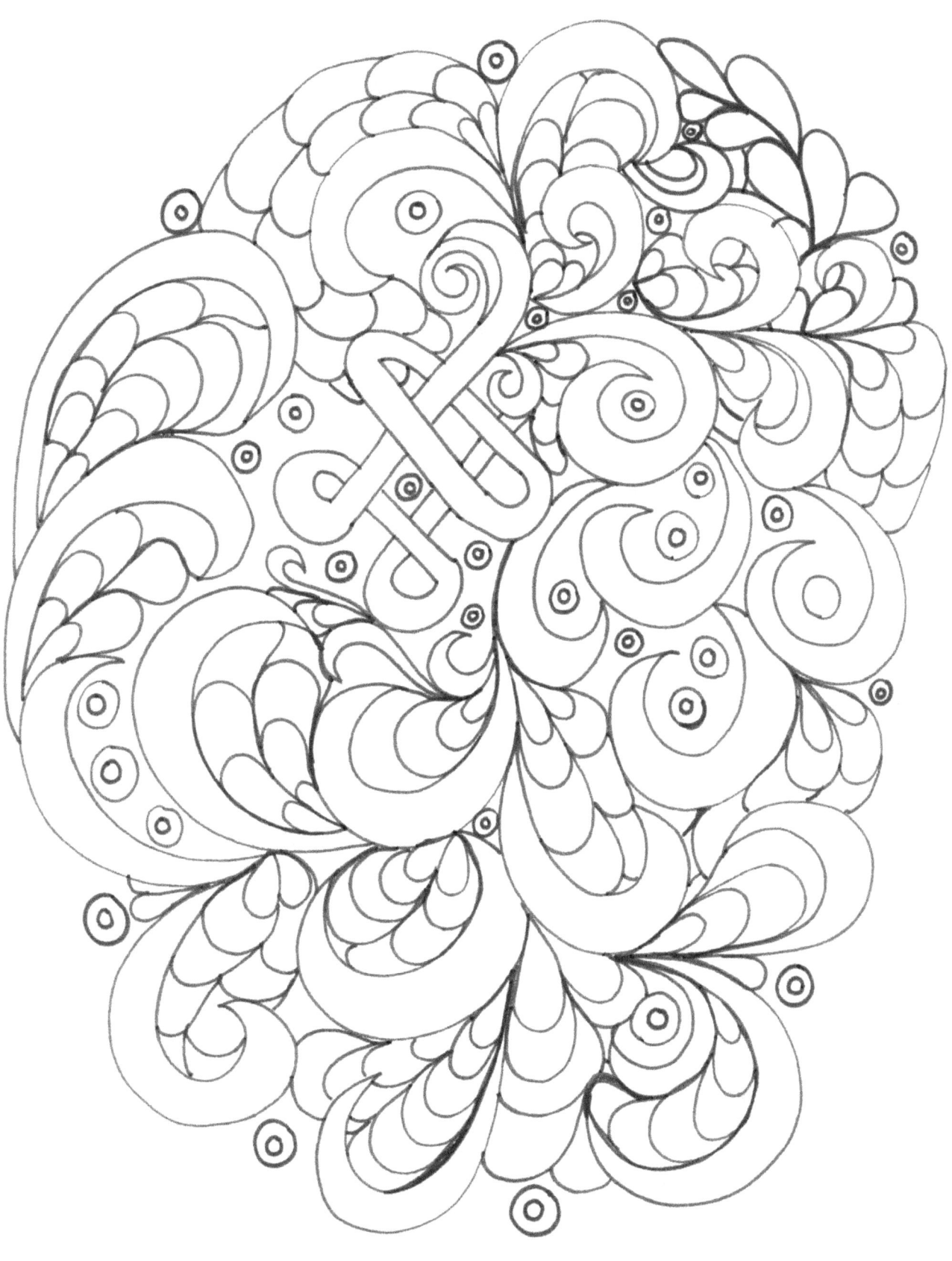

PASSION

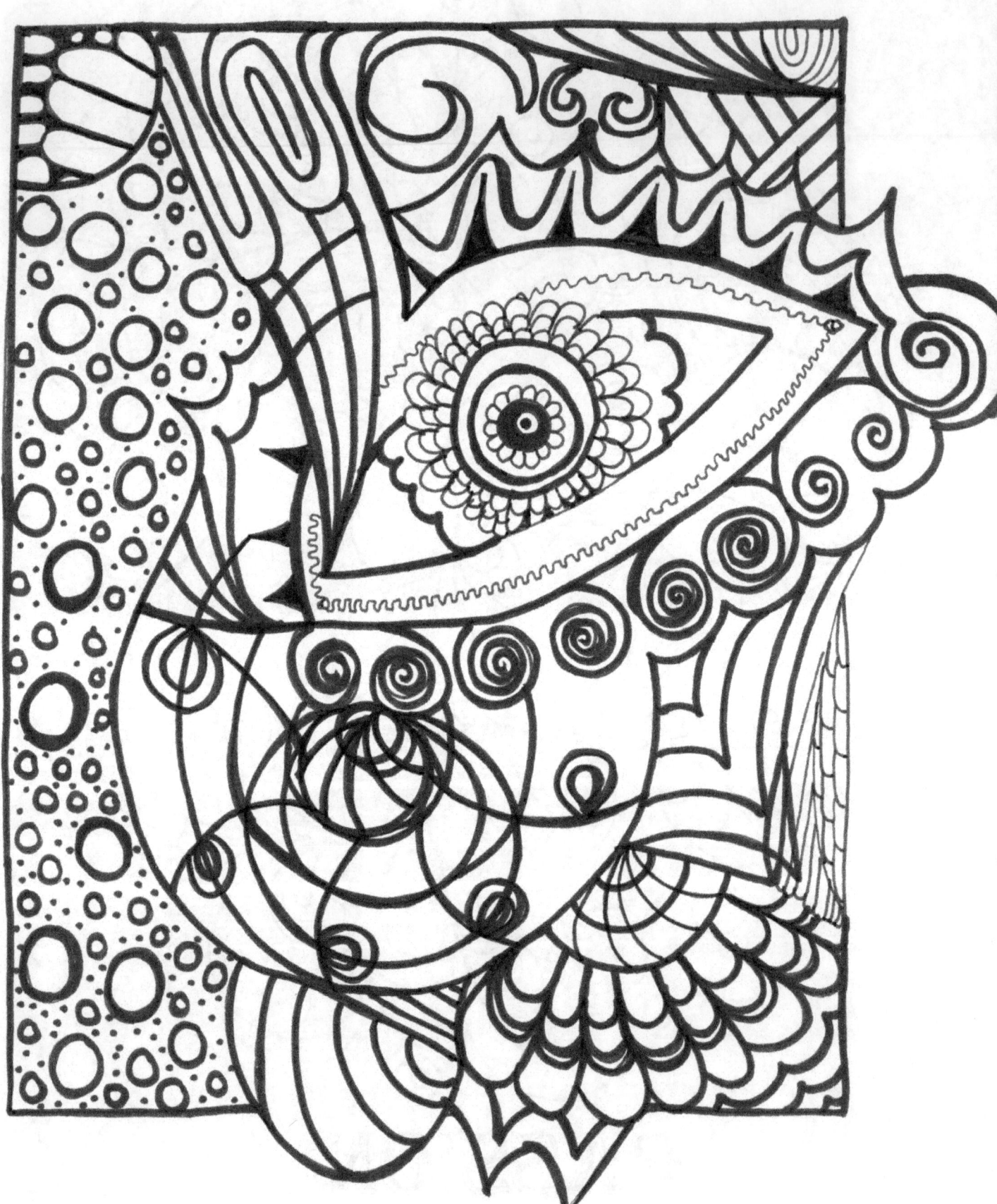

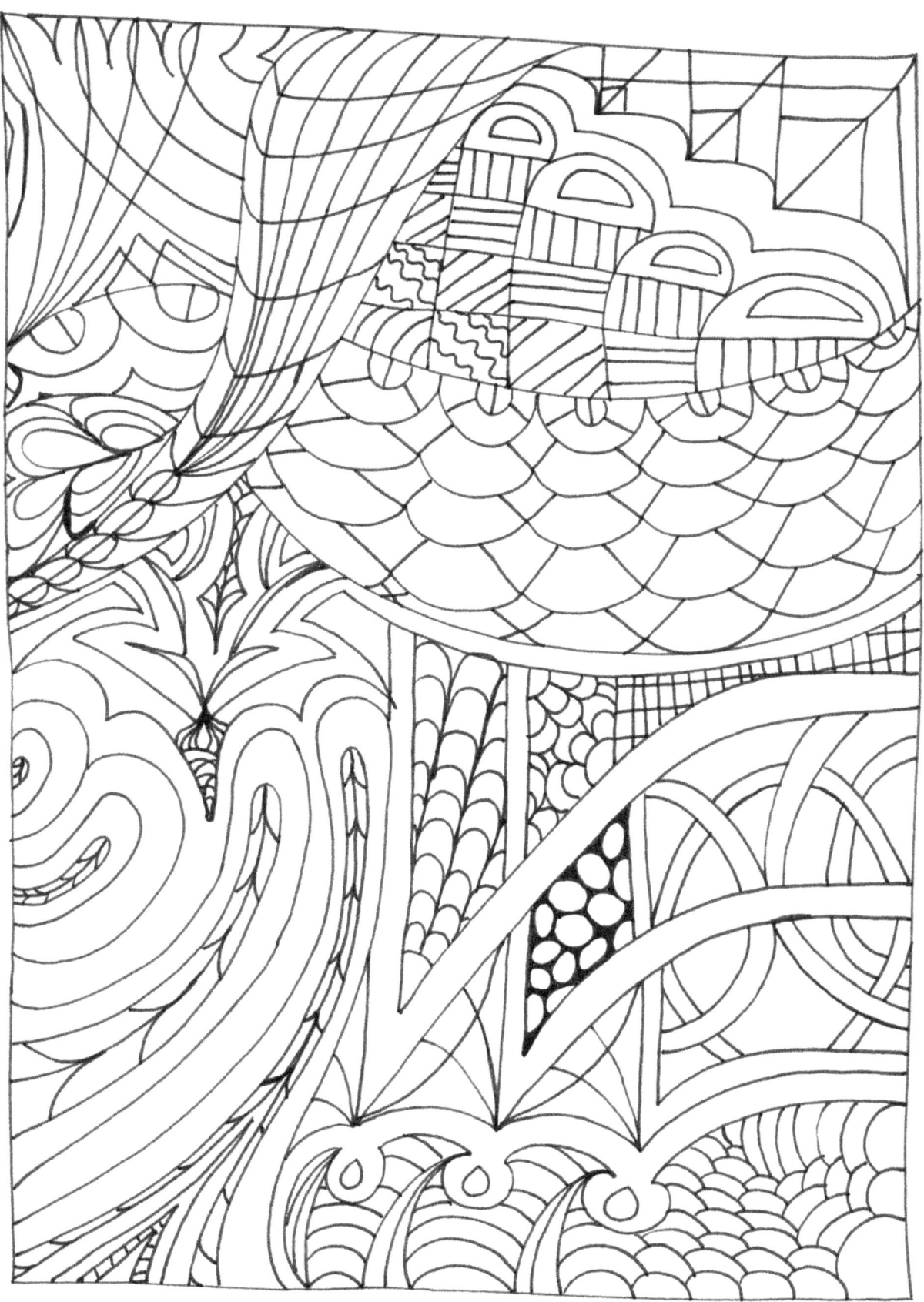

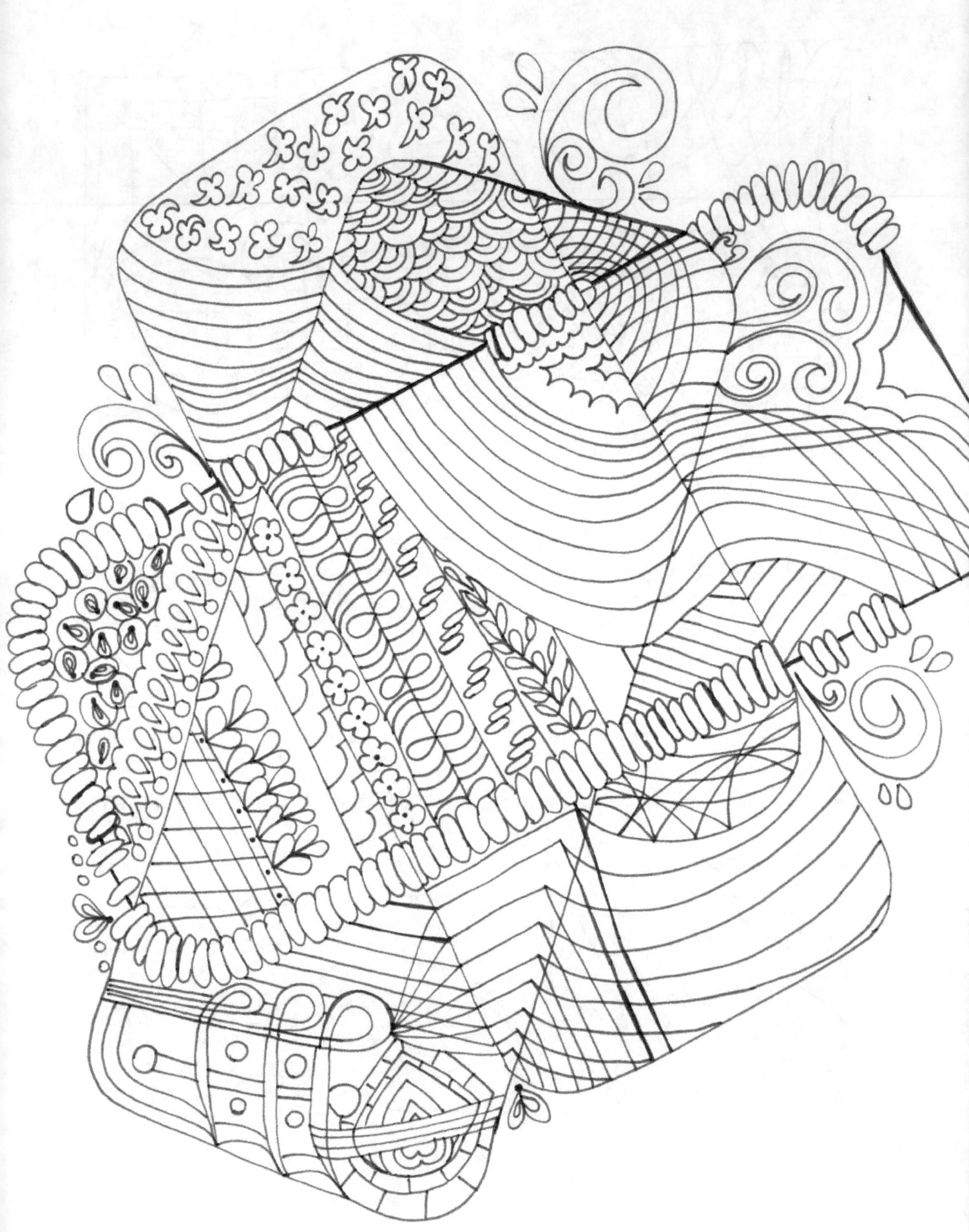

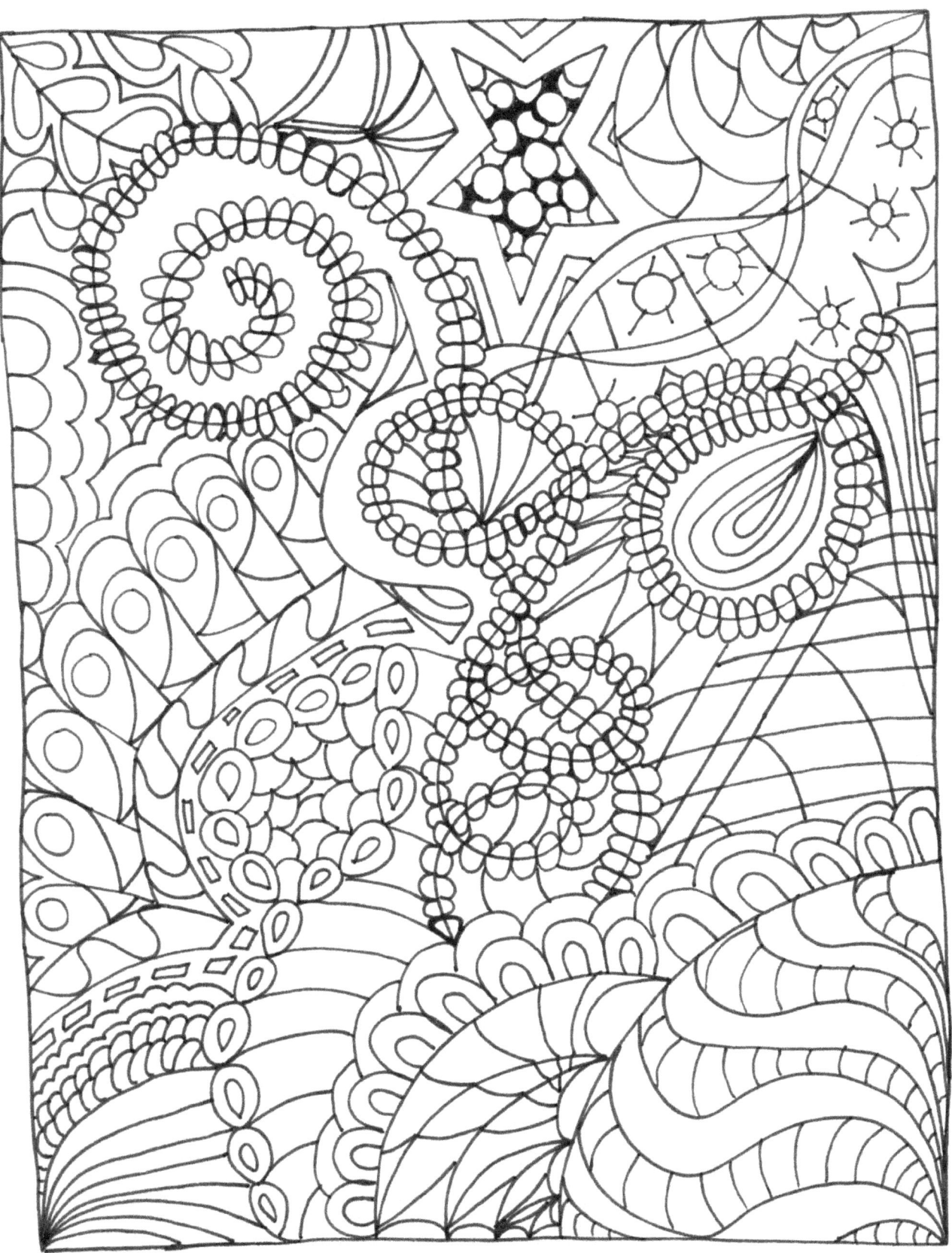

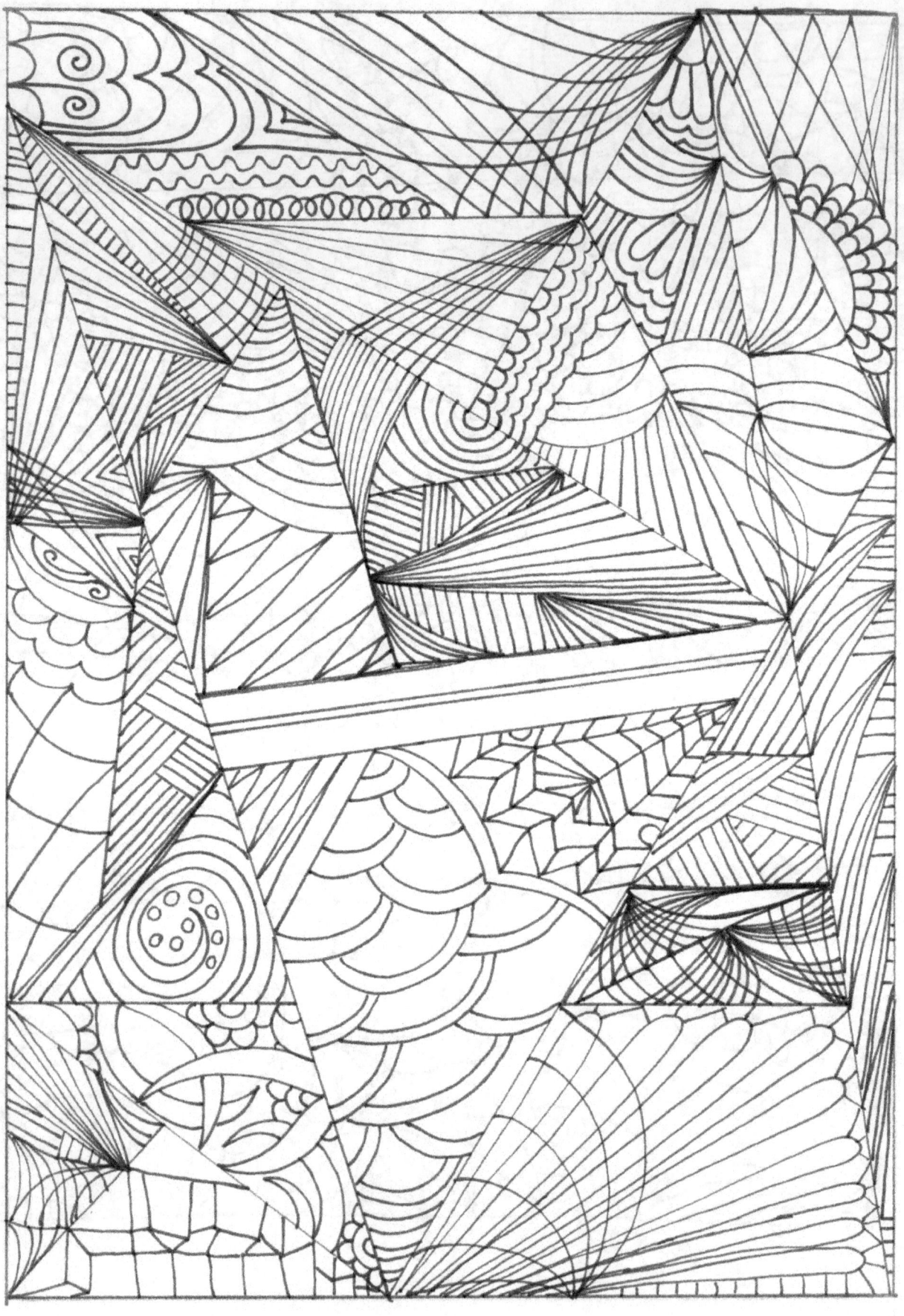

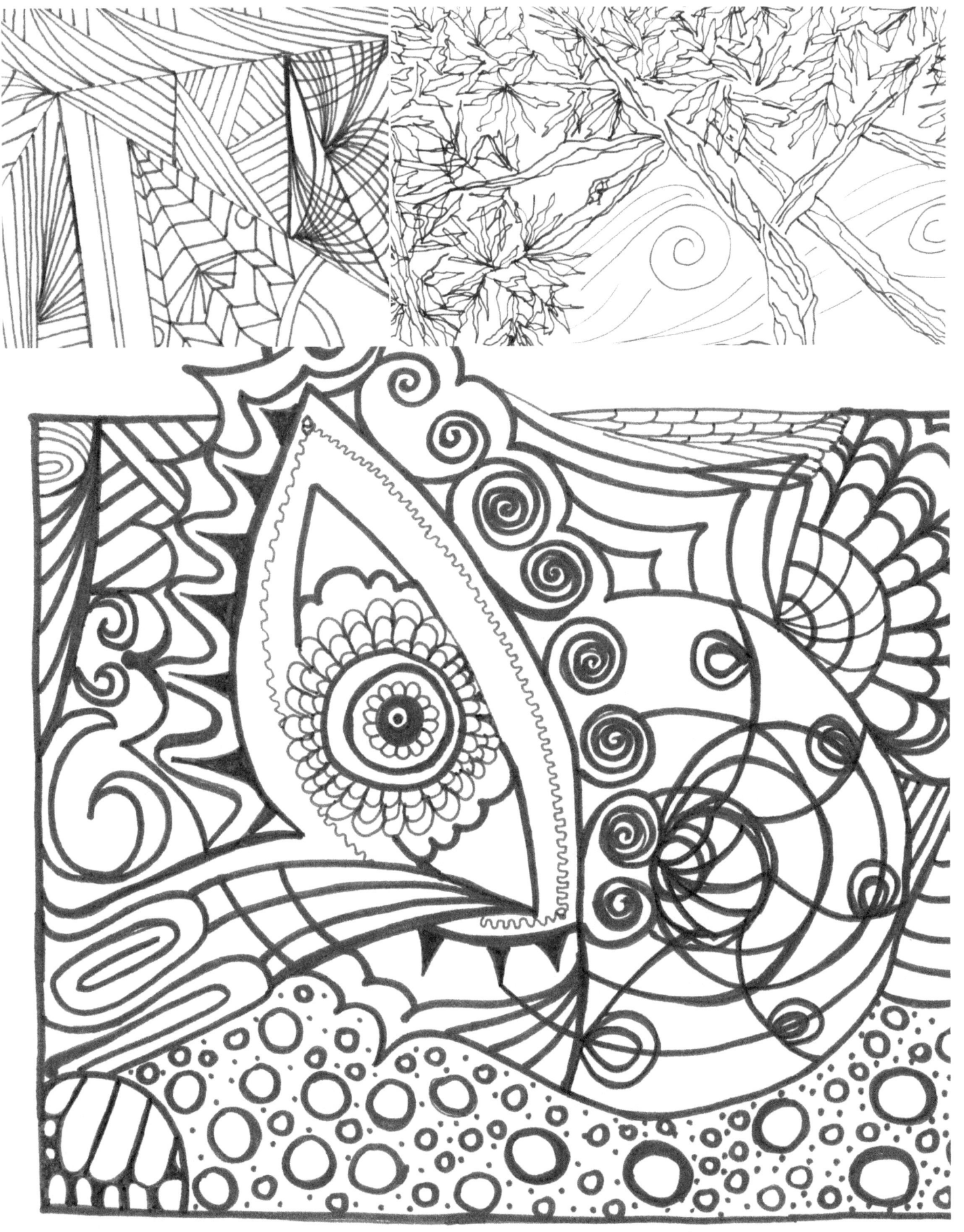

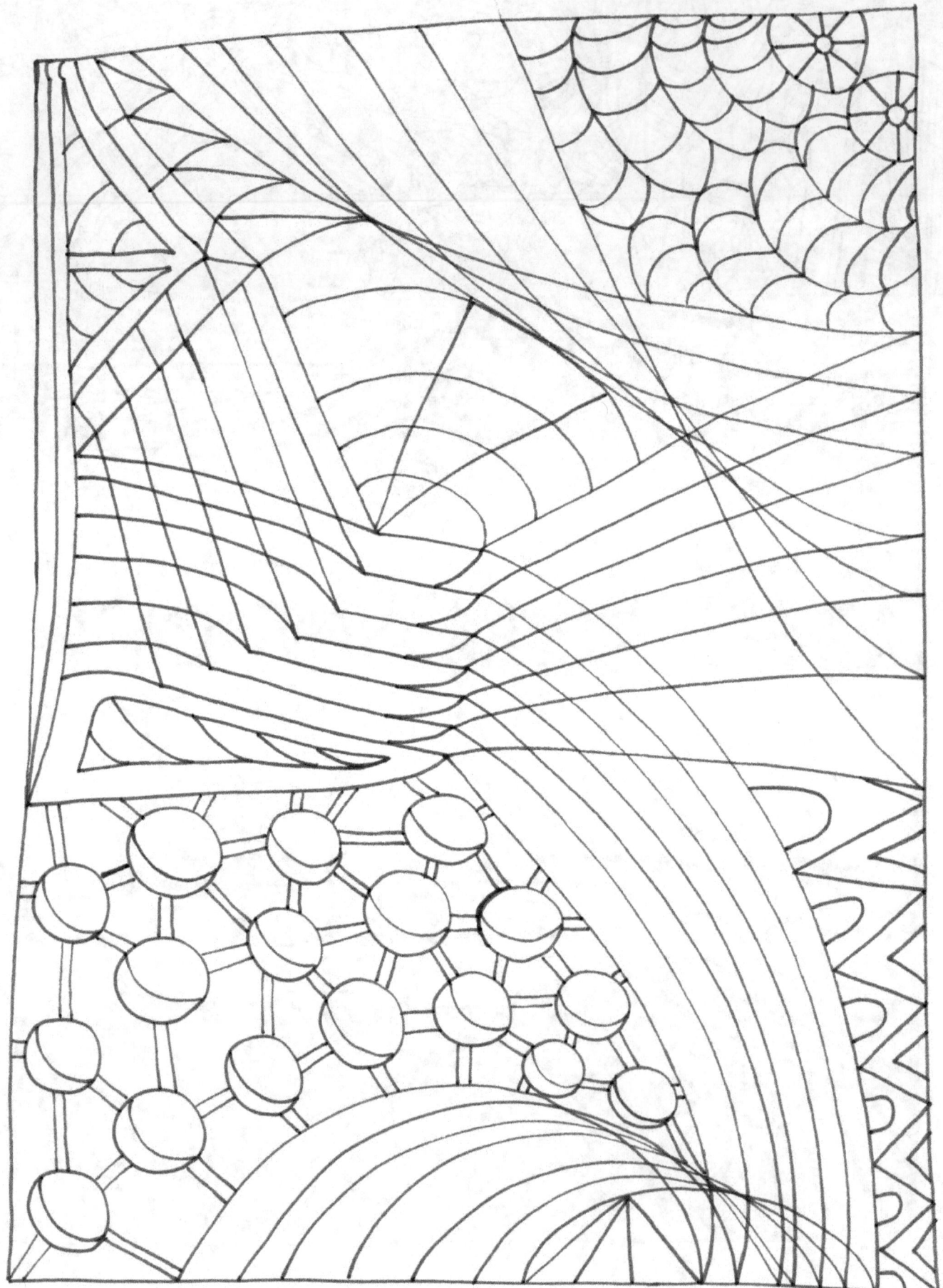

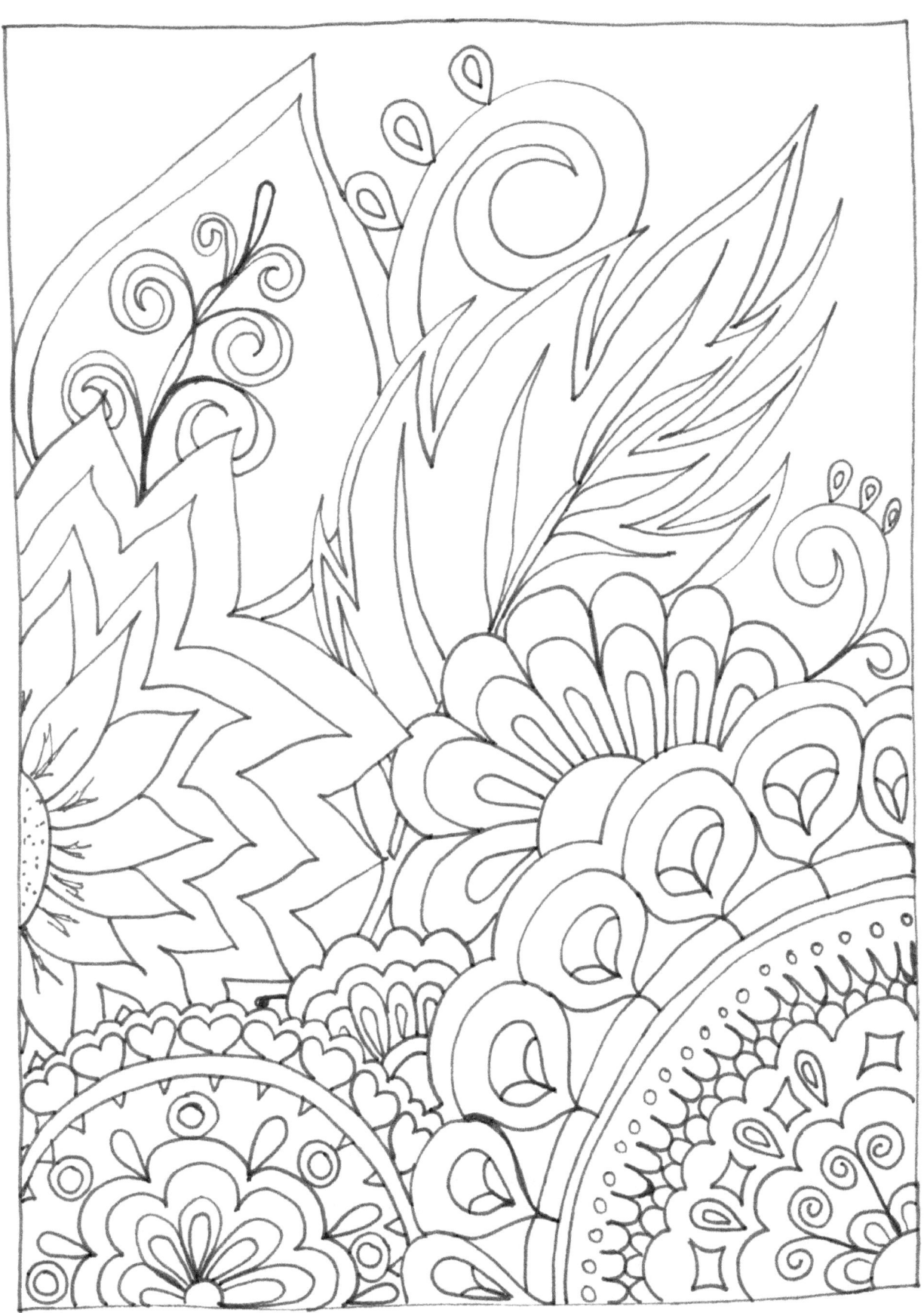

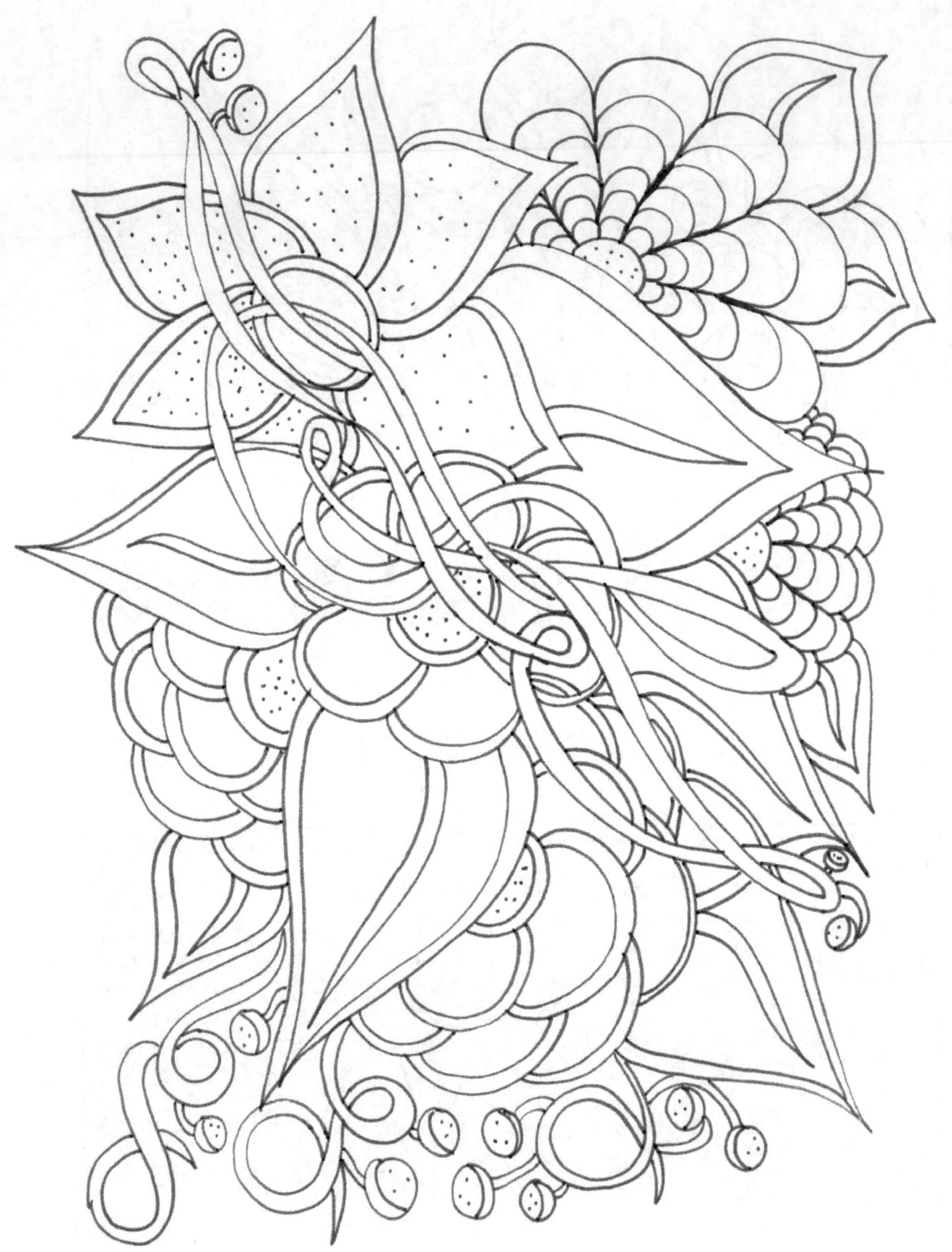

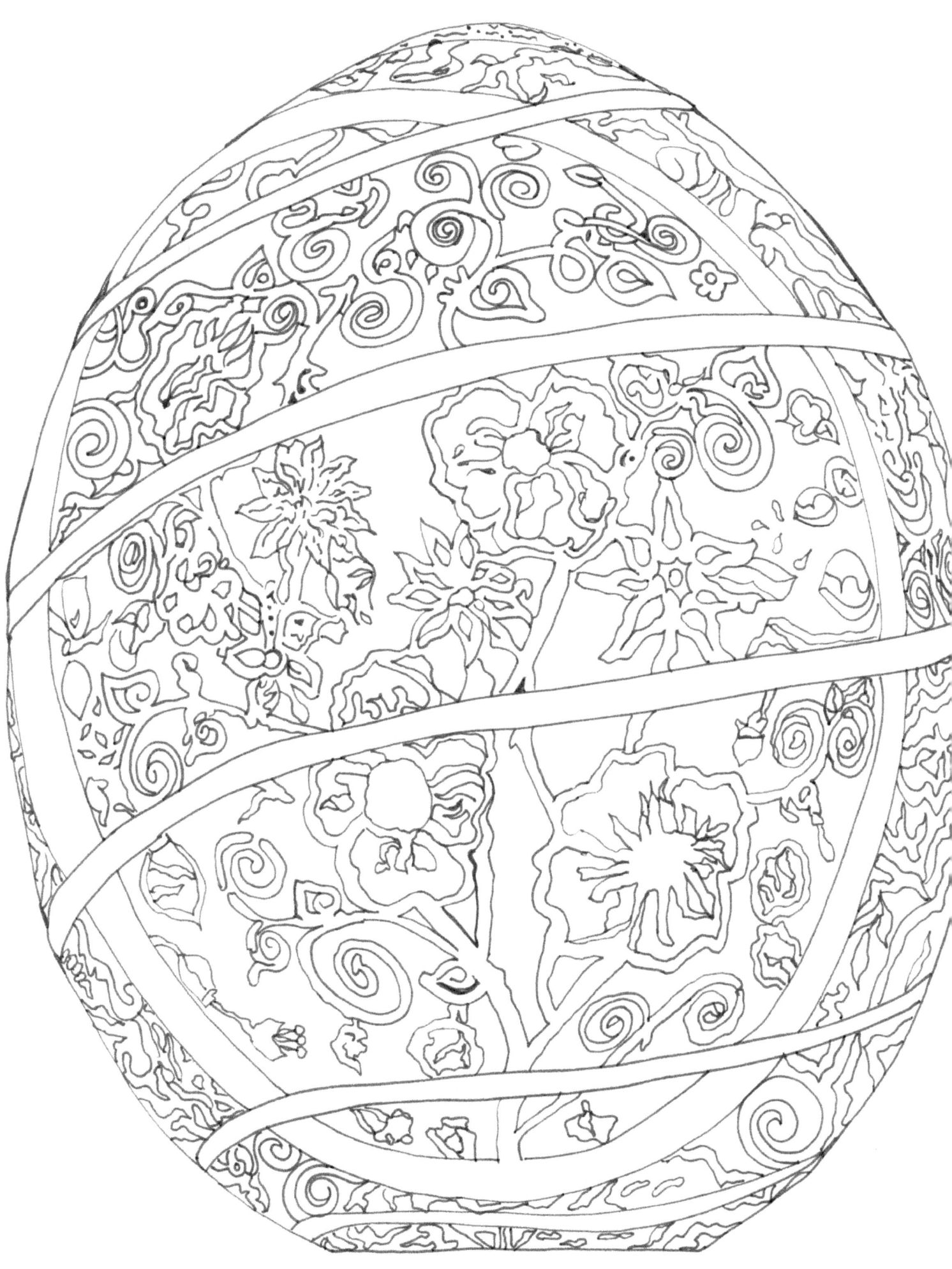

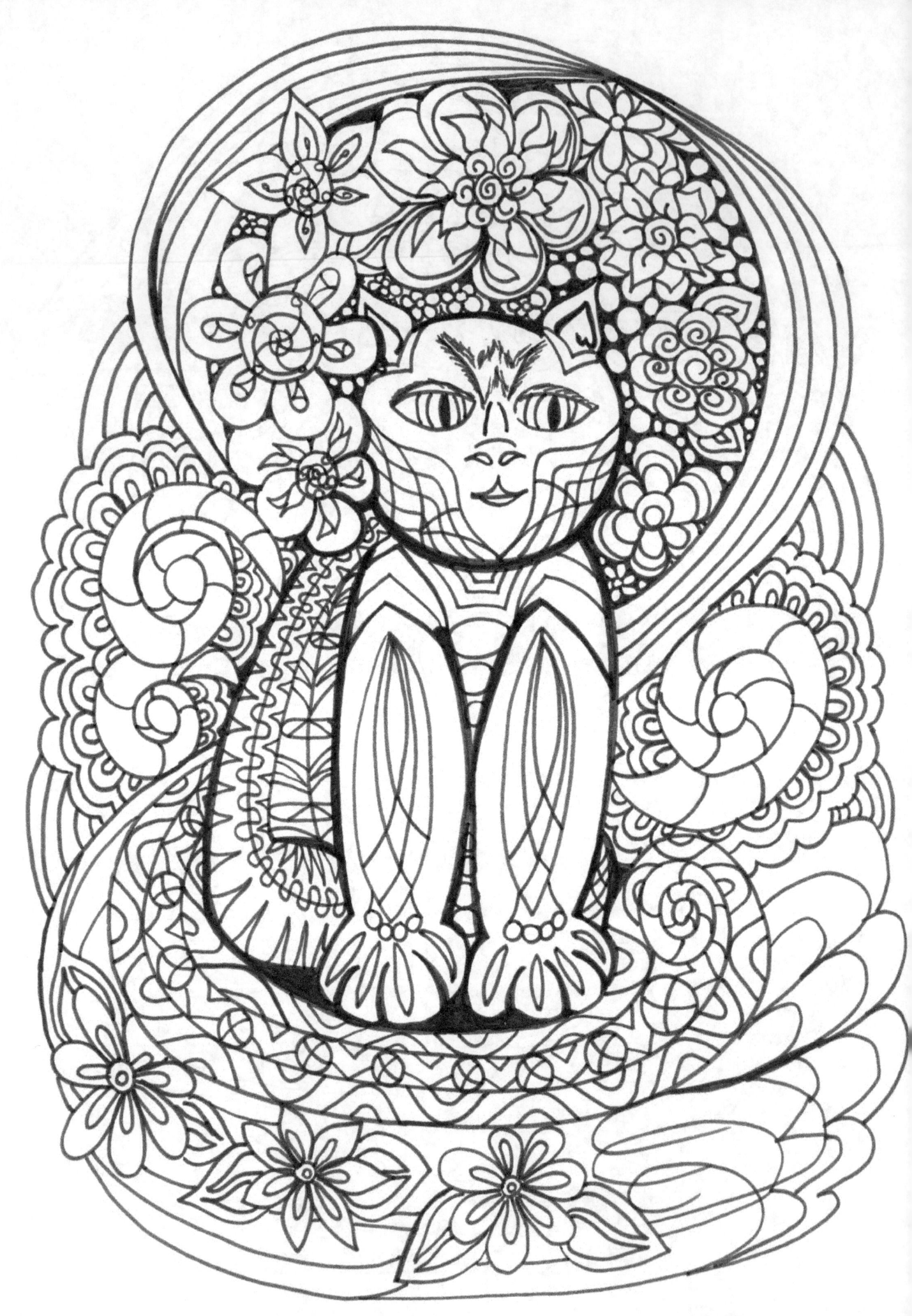

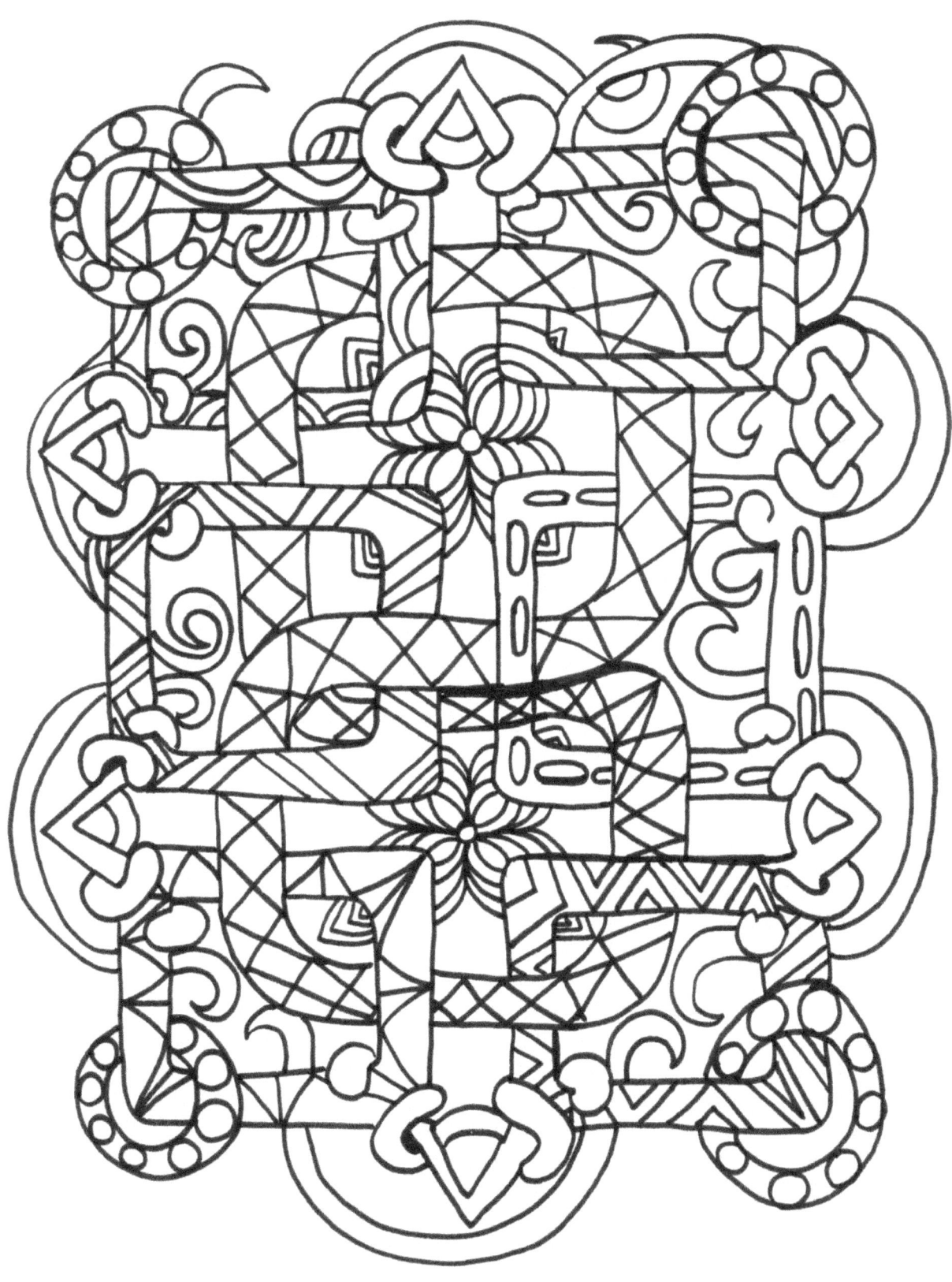

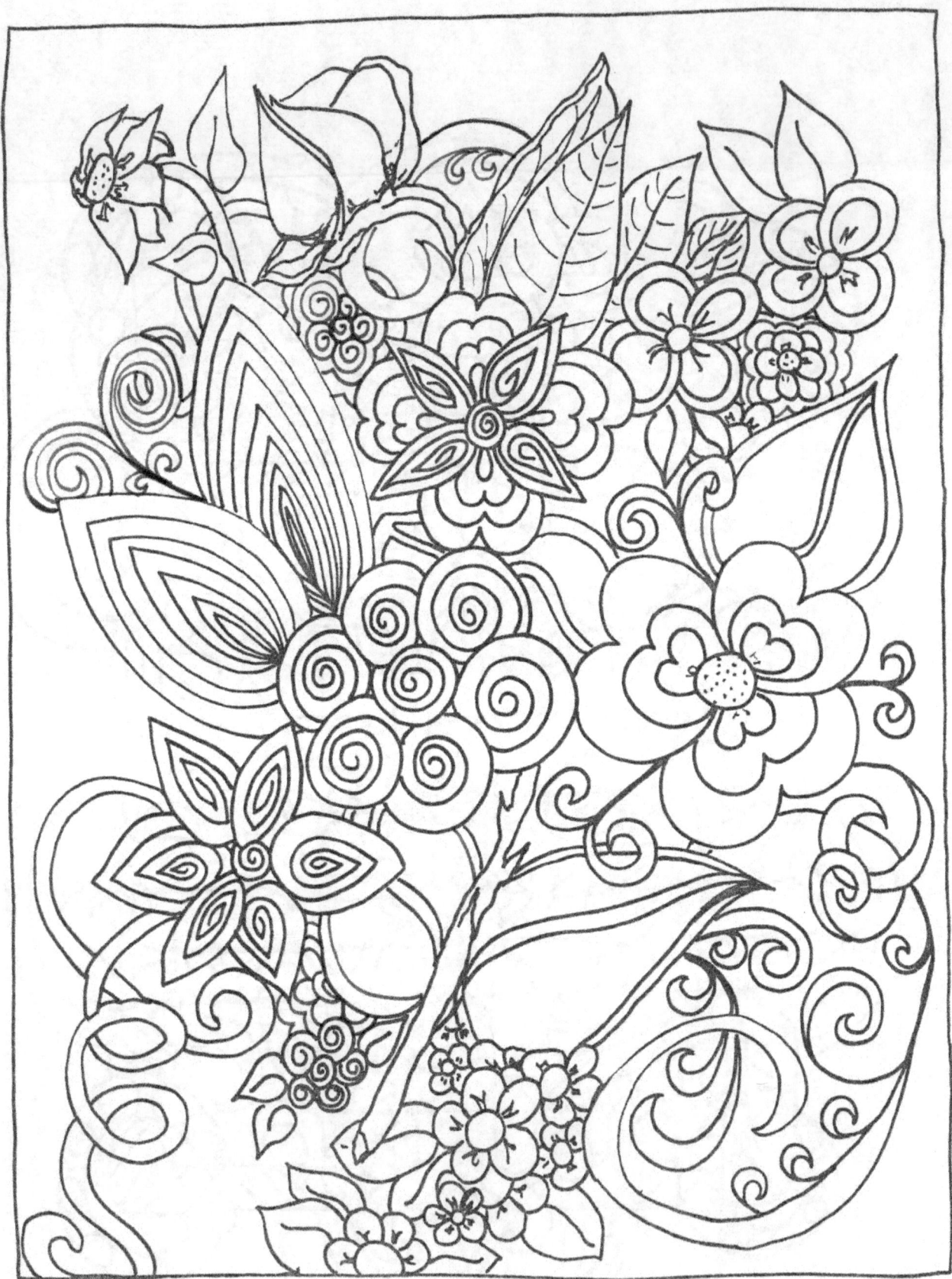

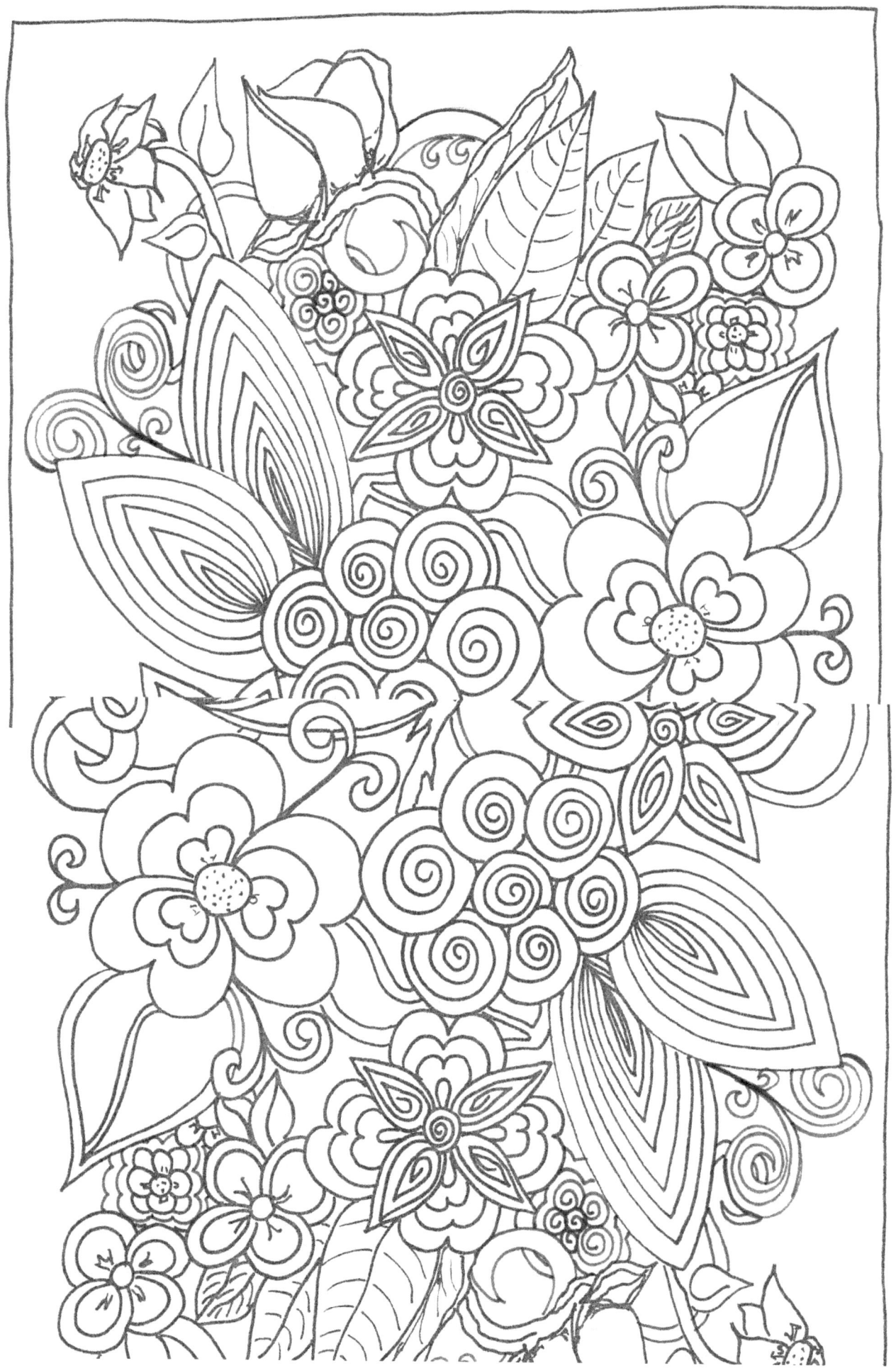

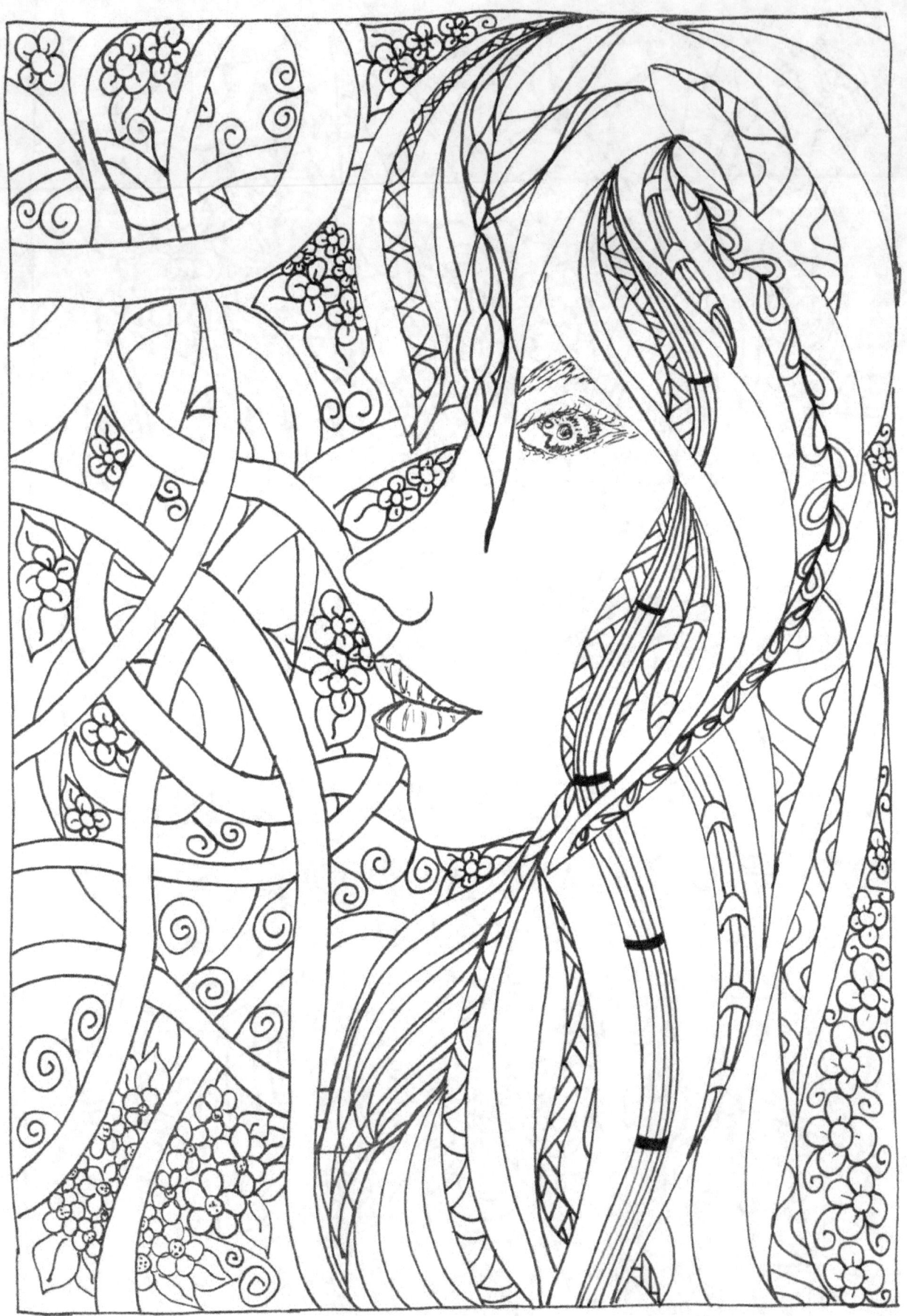

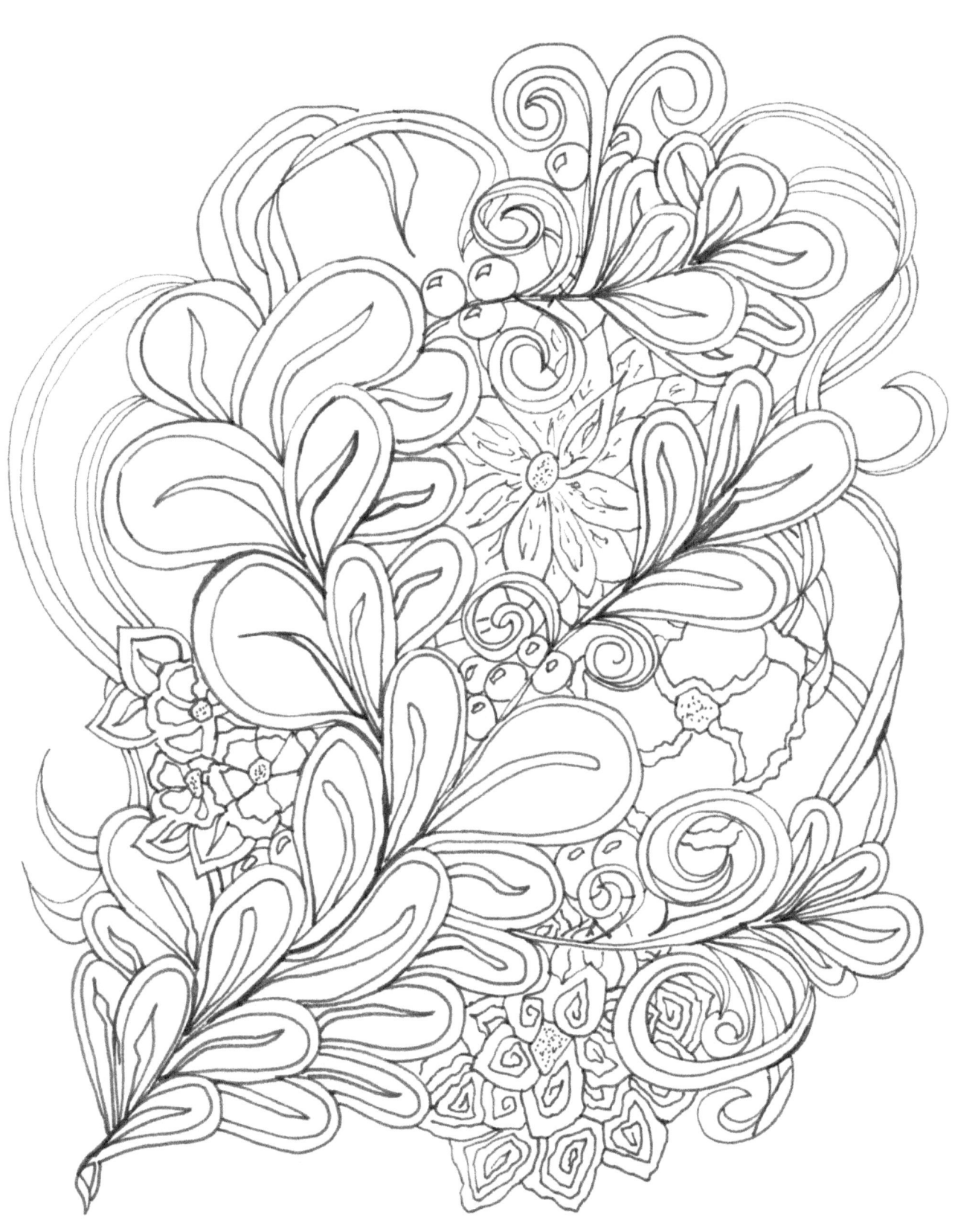

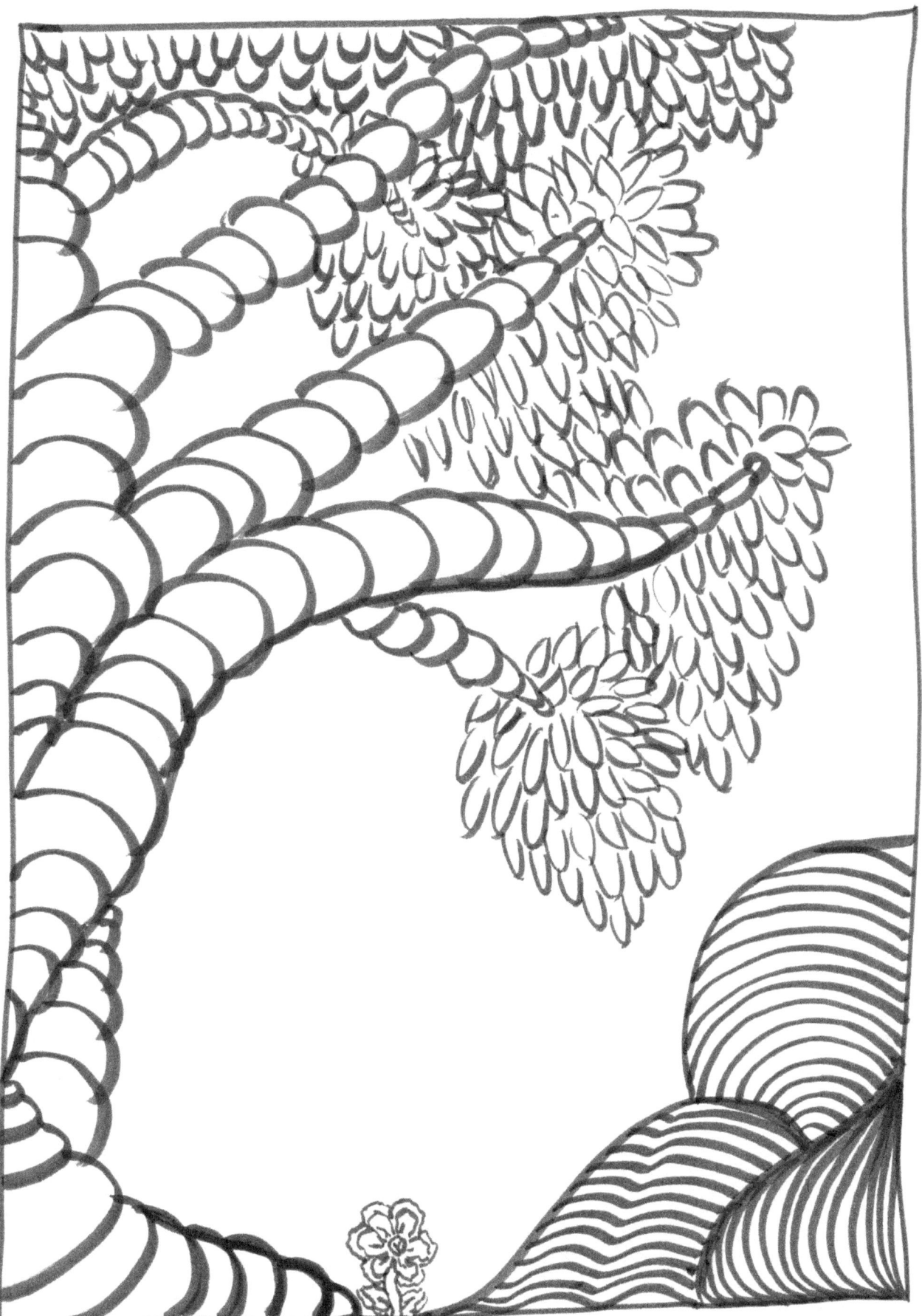

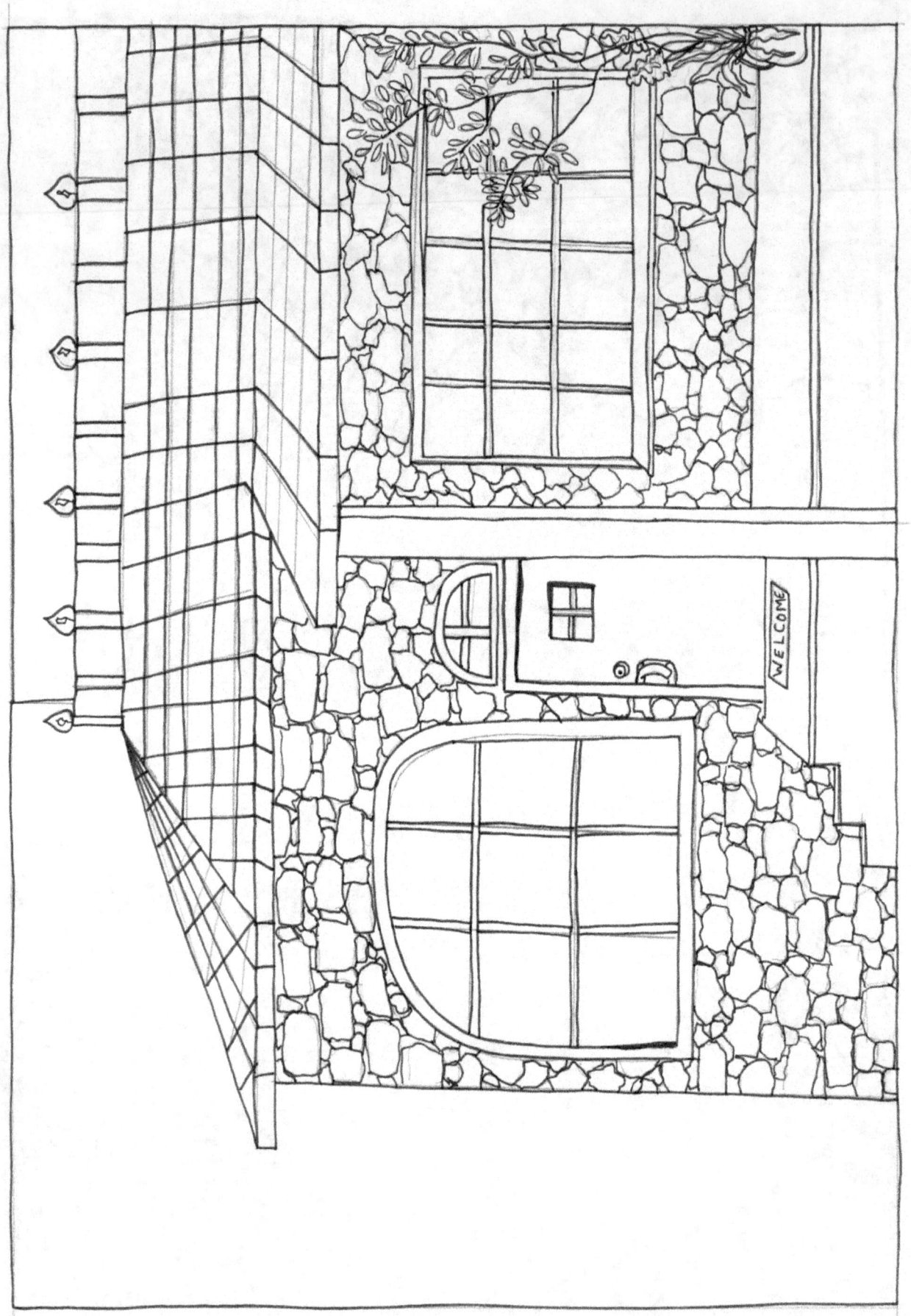

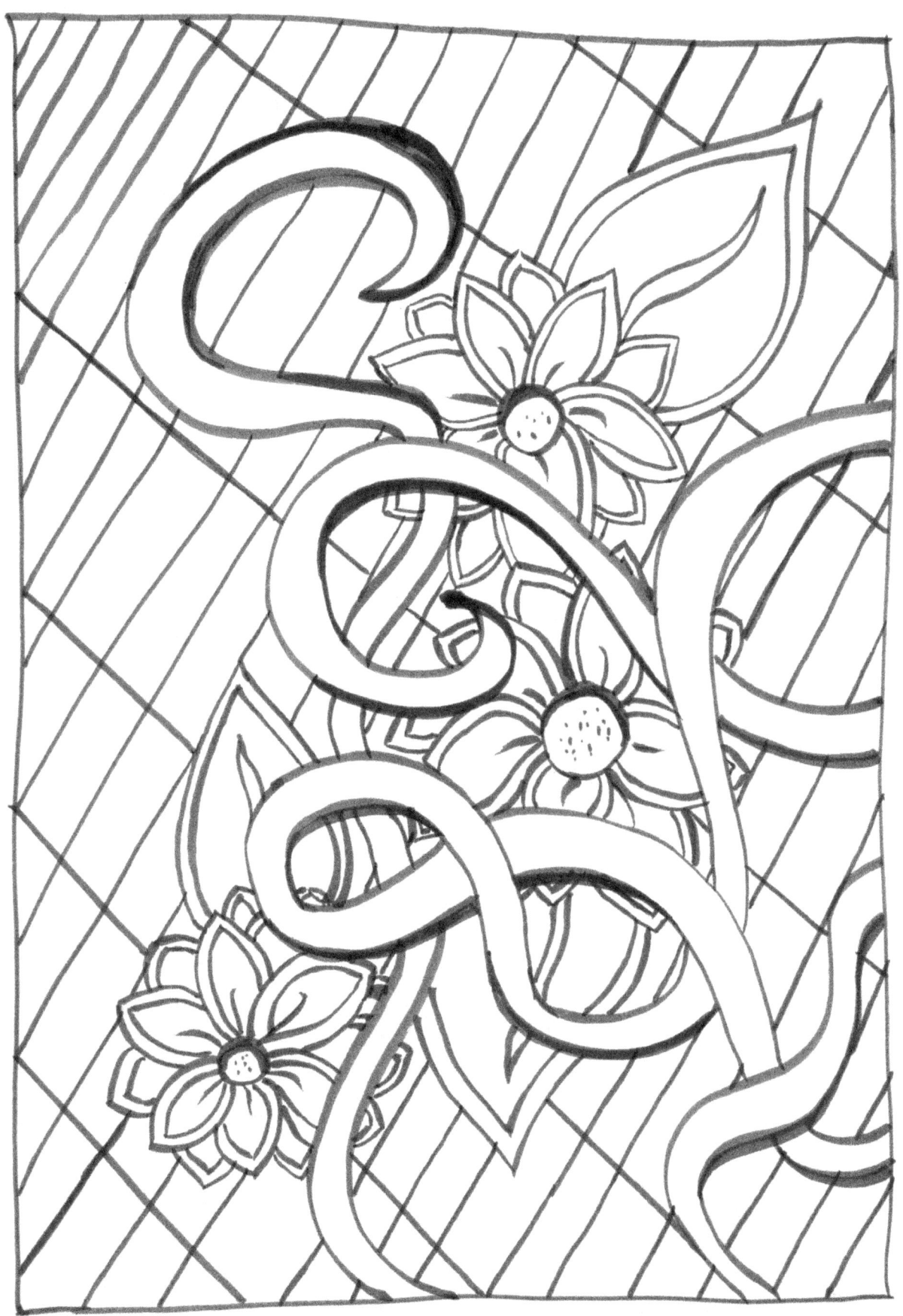

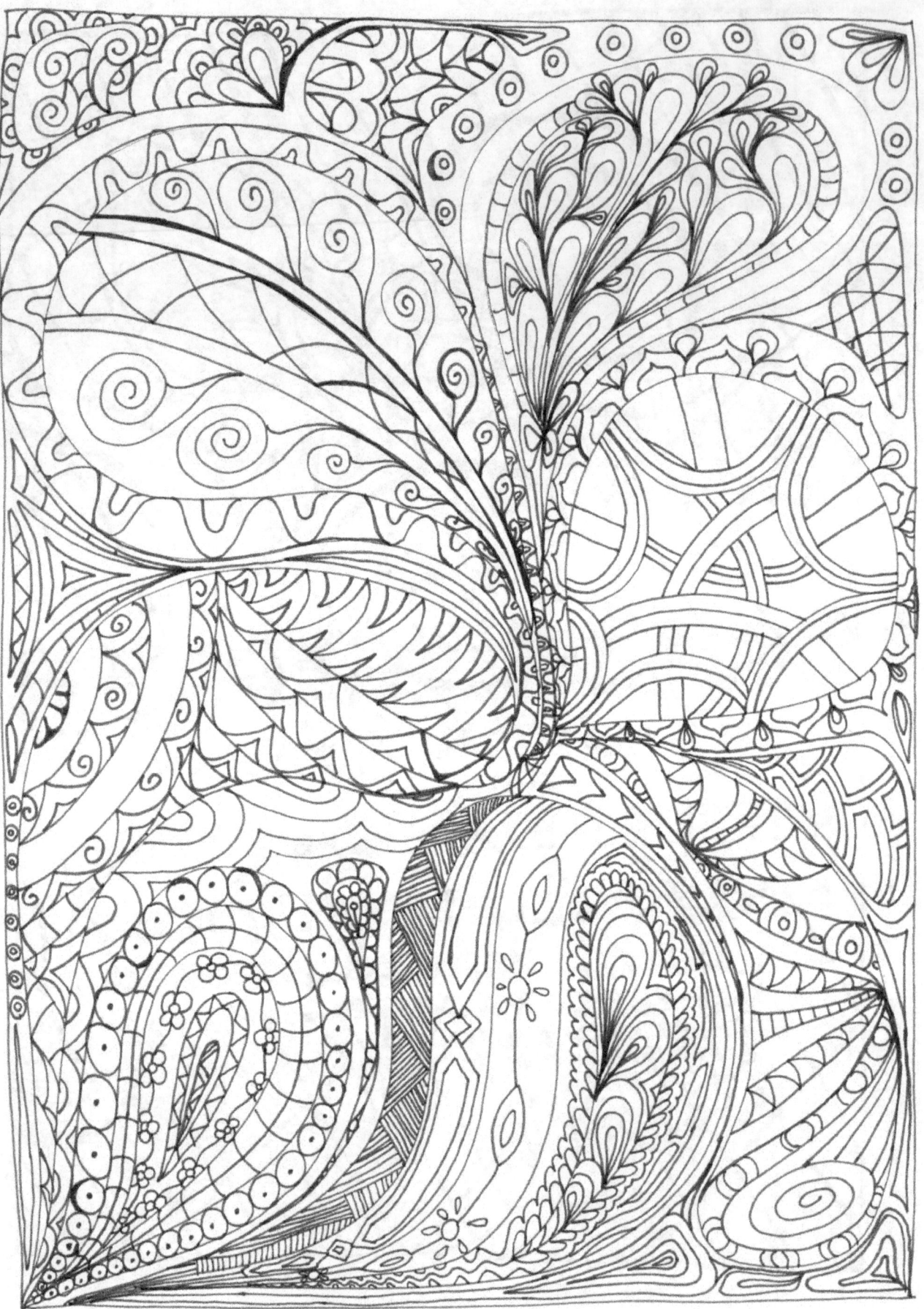

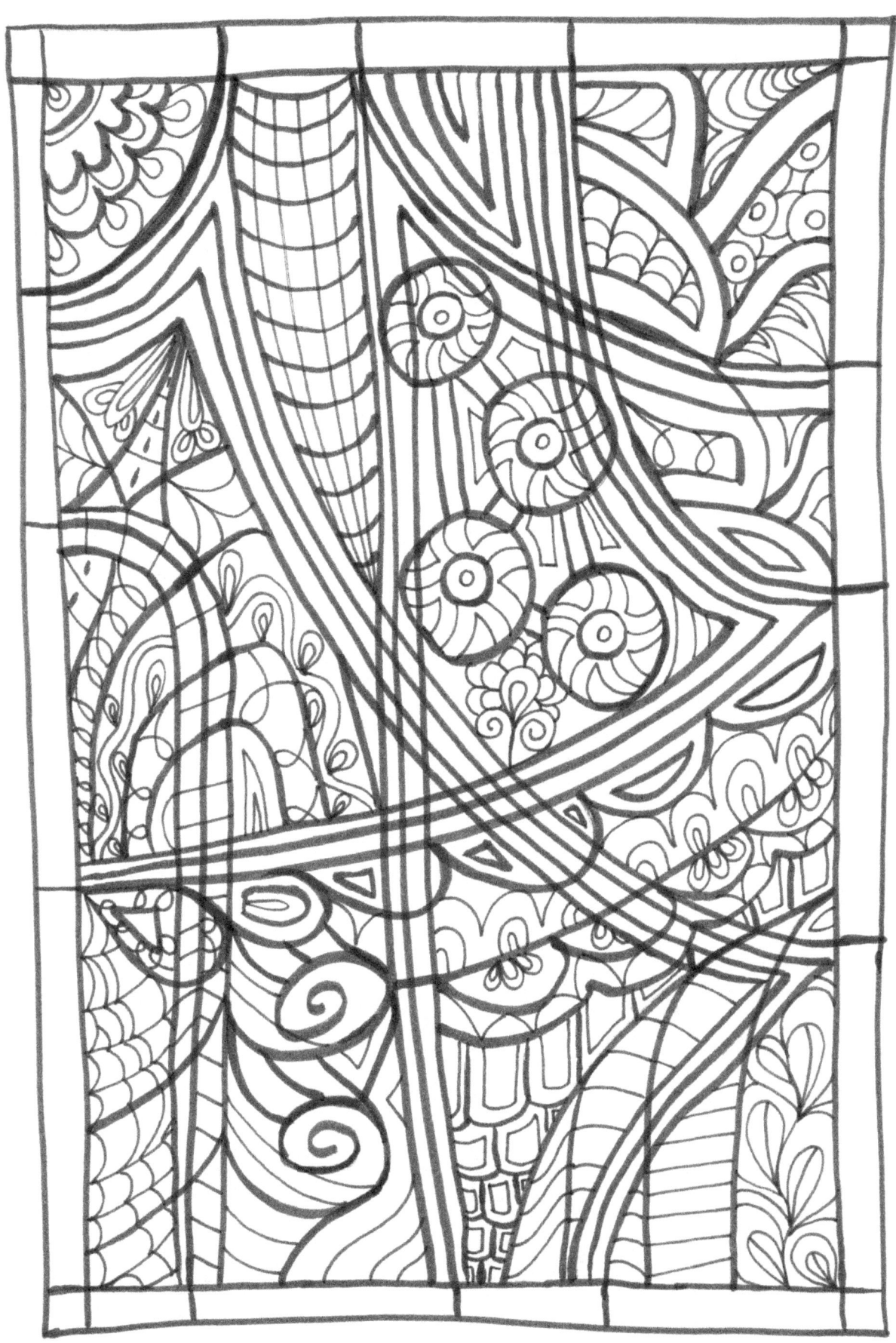

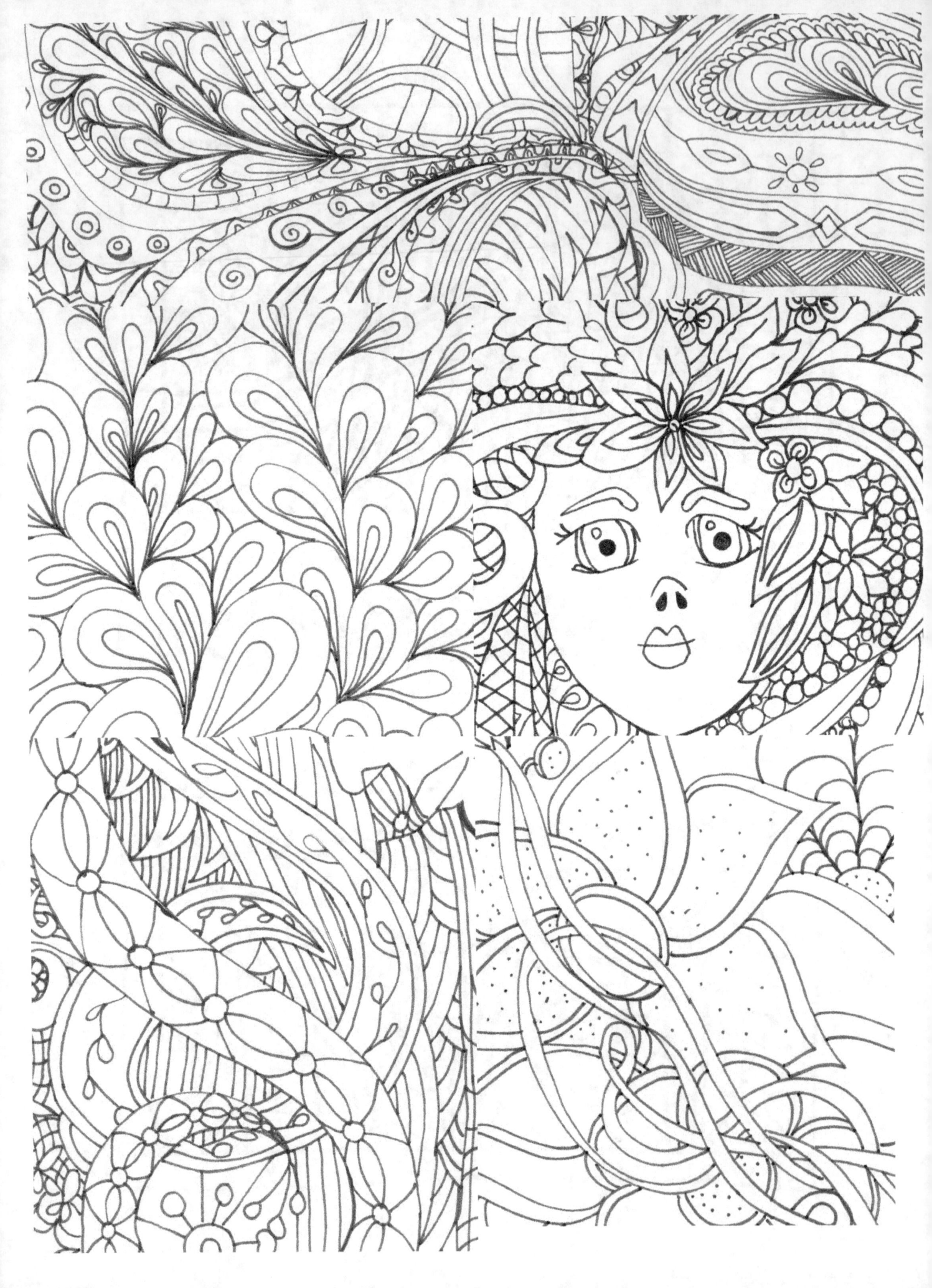

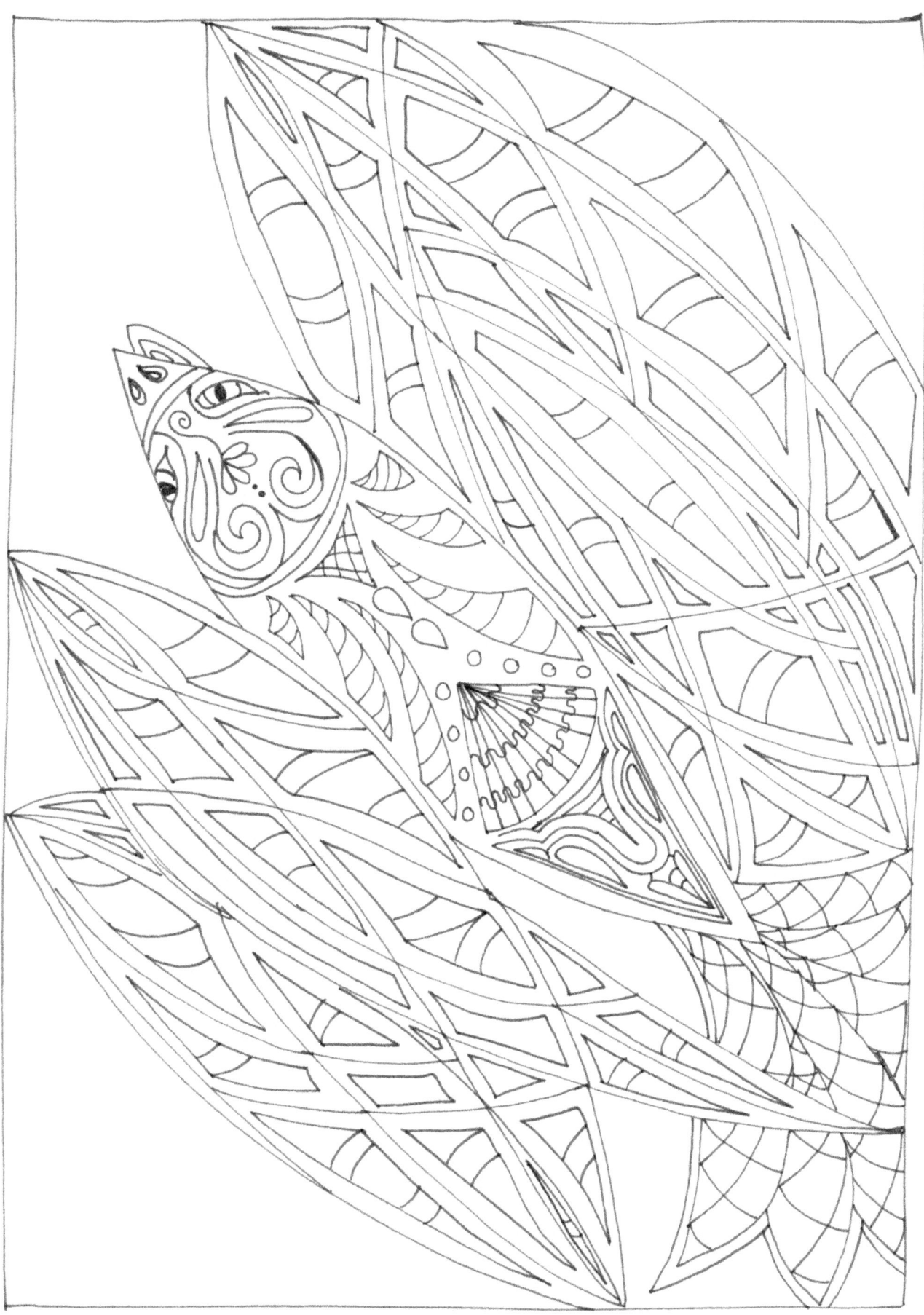

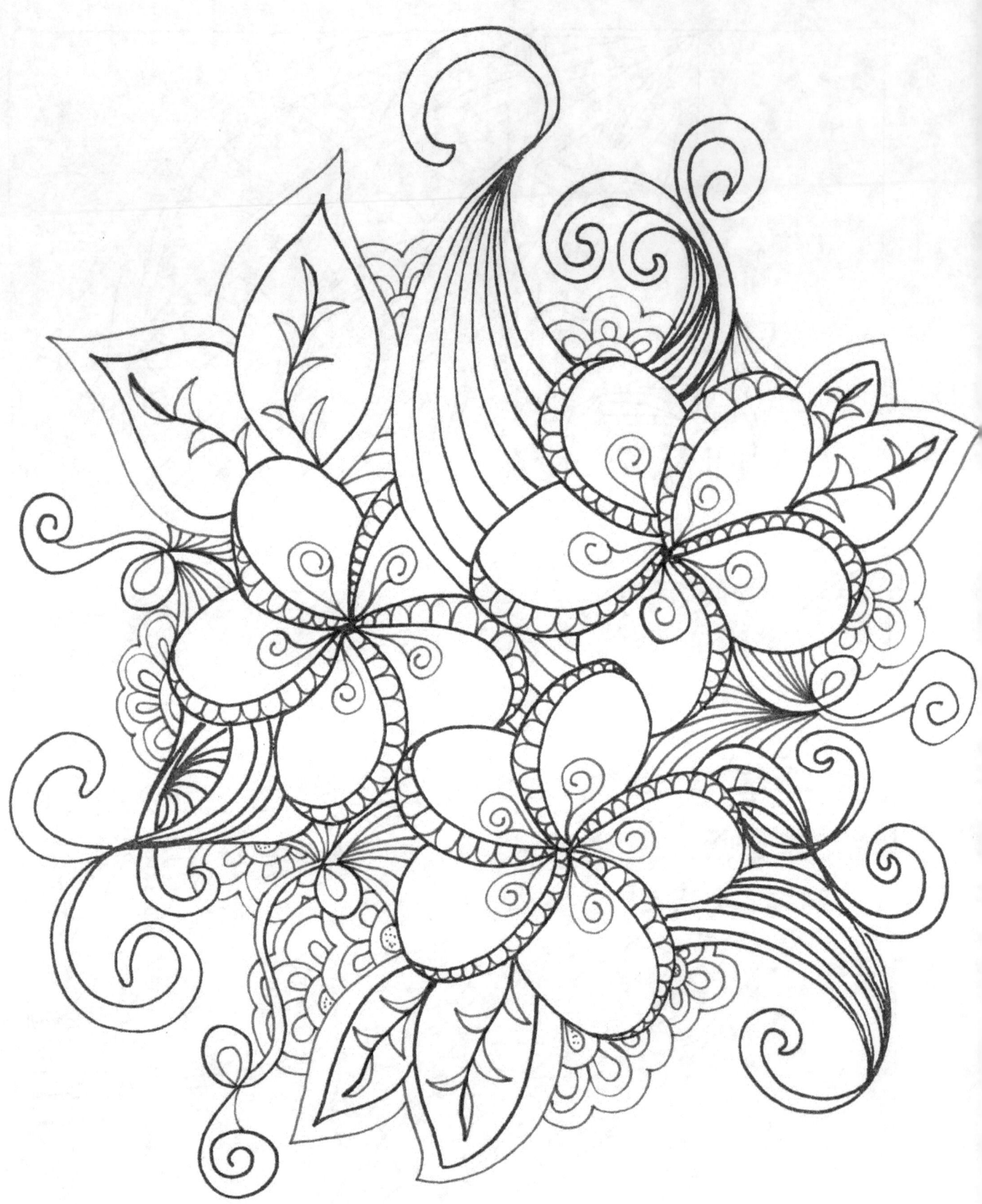

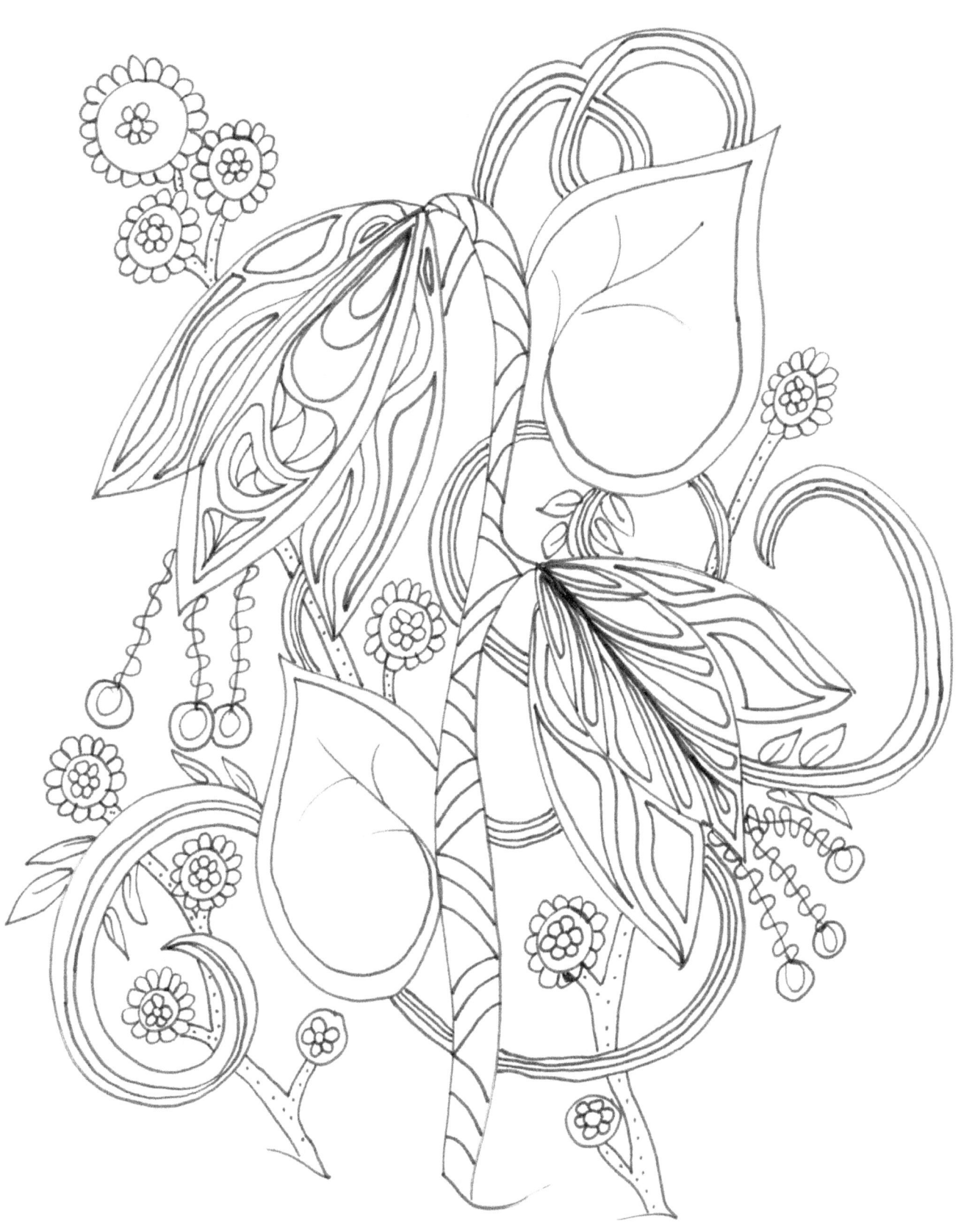

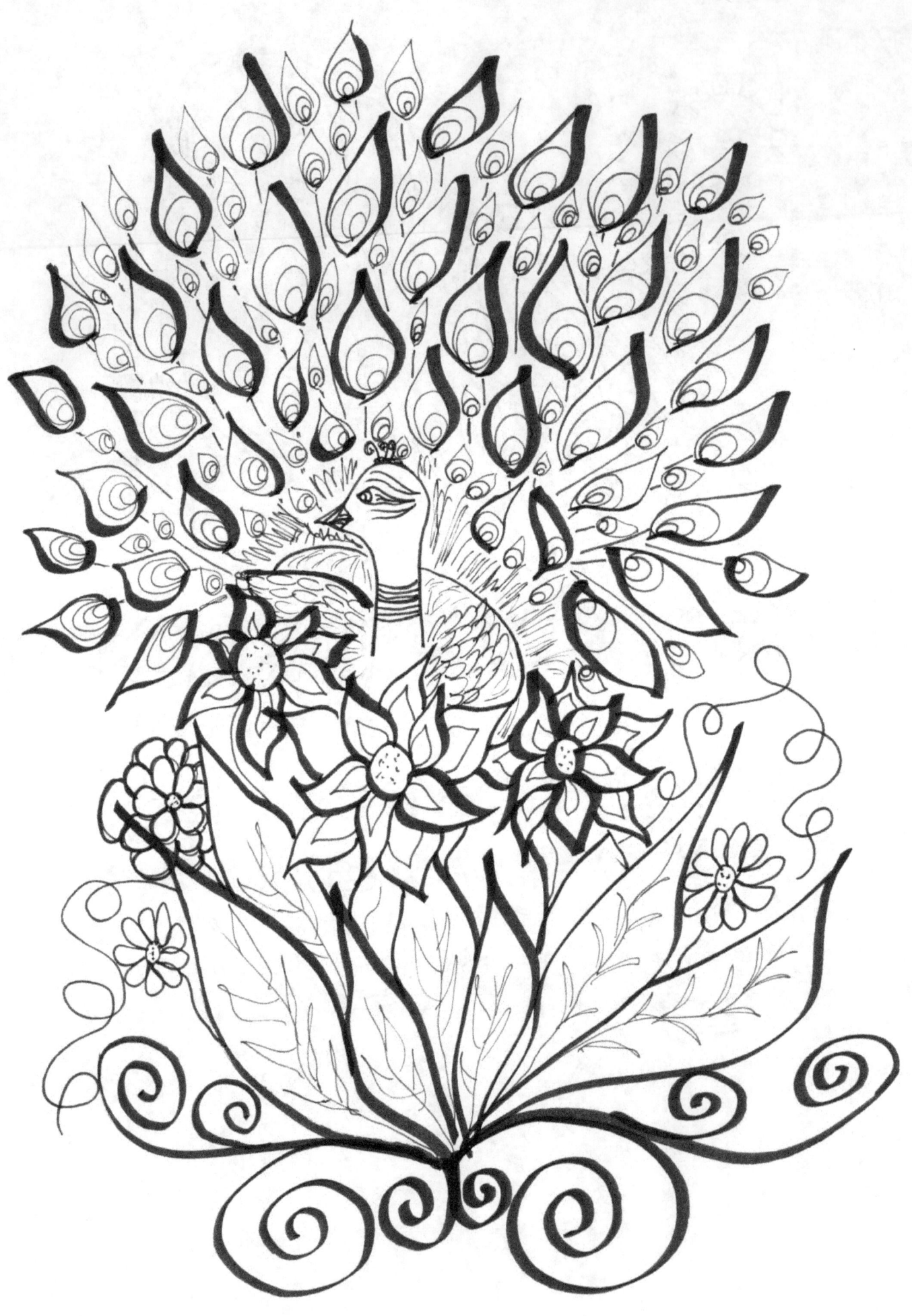

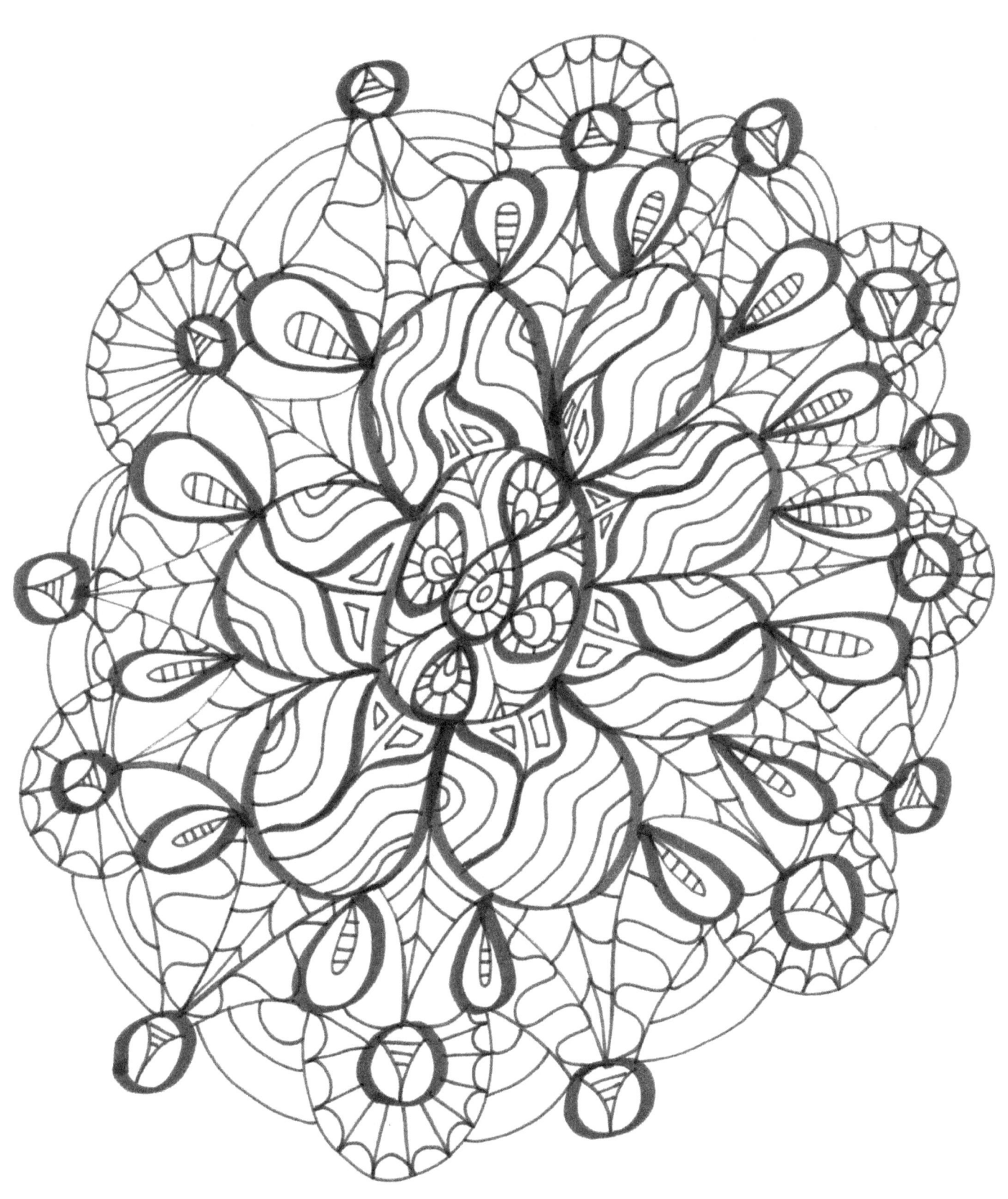

Create a Zentangle rose on this page, you can use any colors that you like.

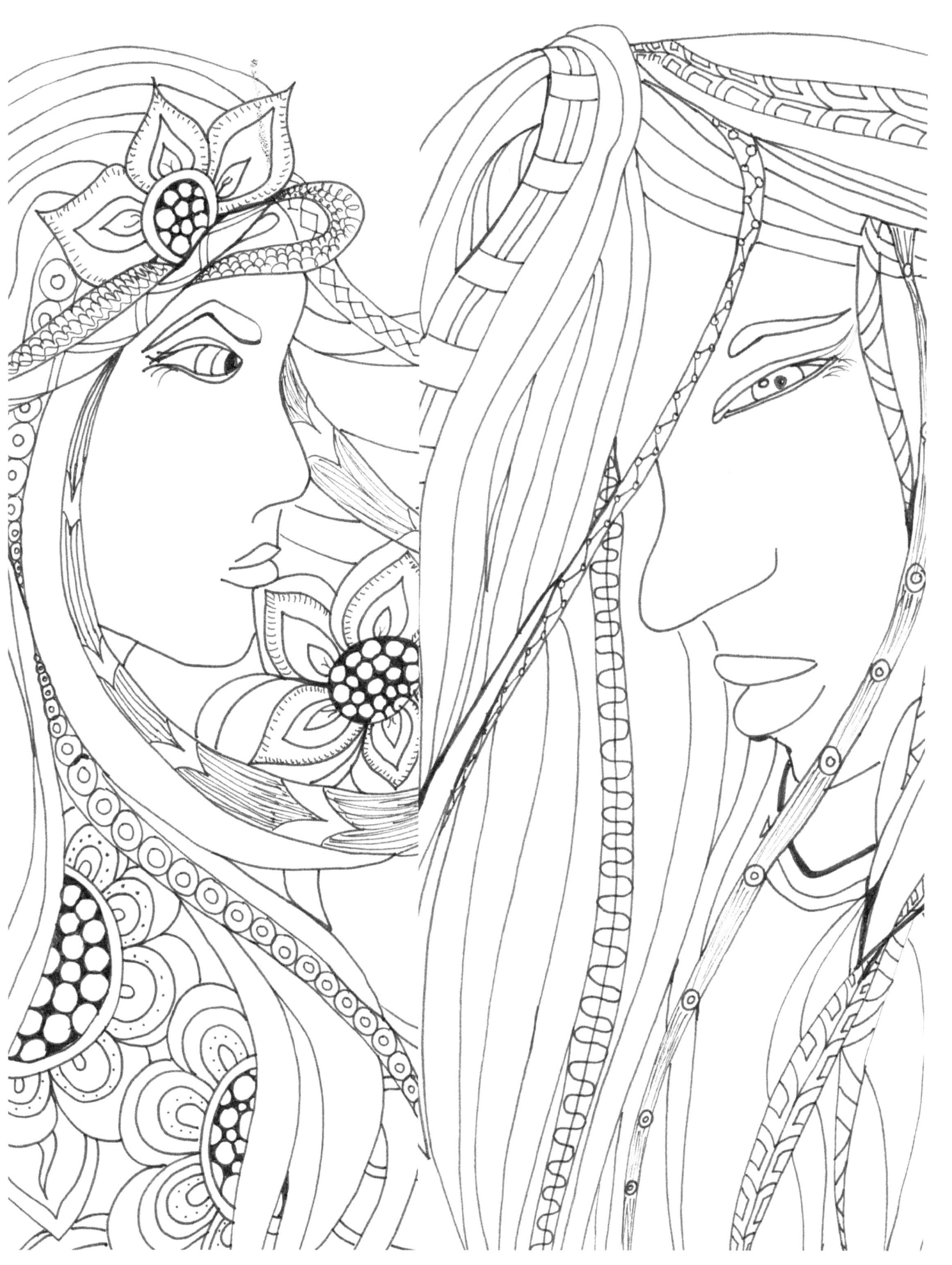

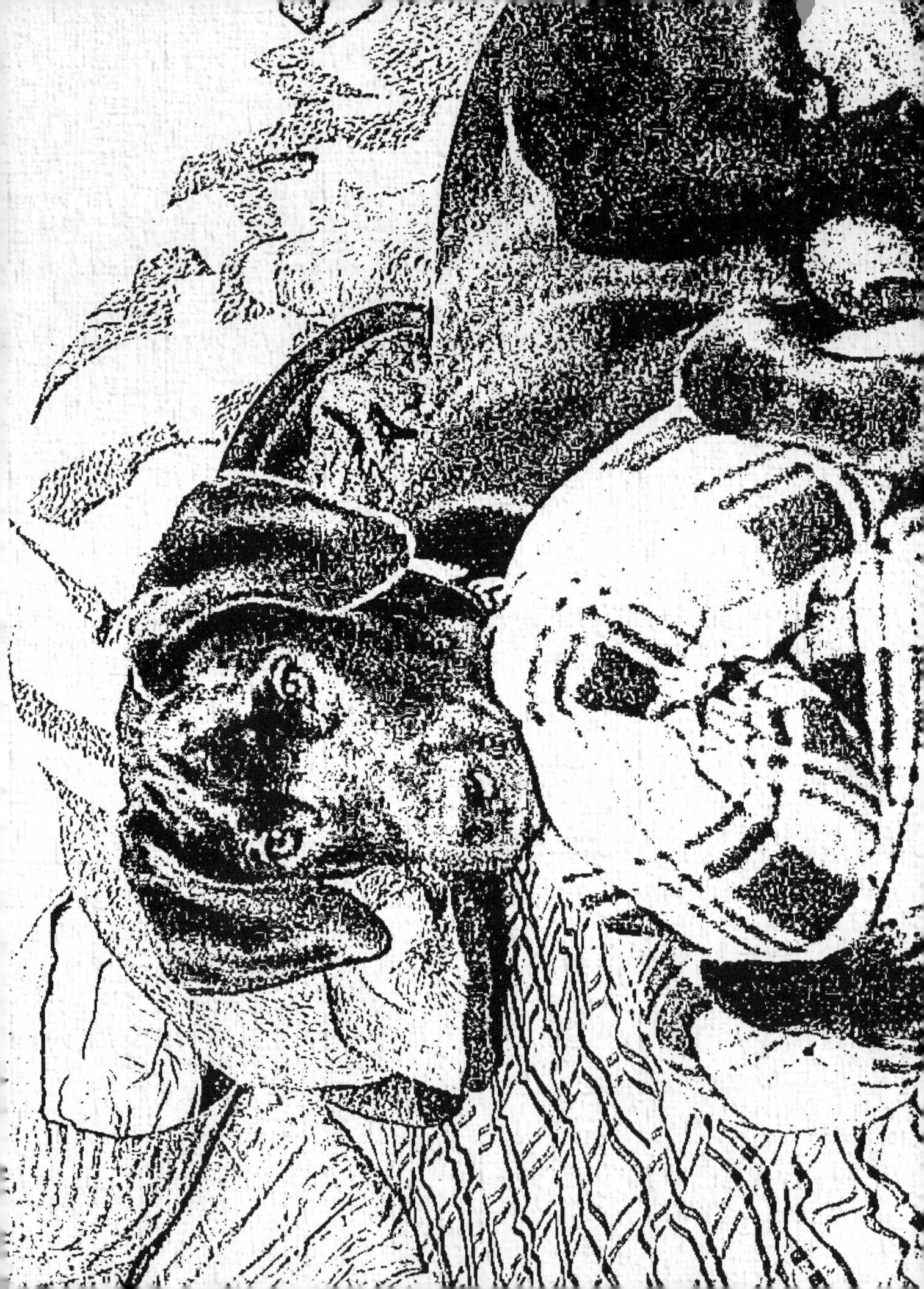